The Adventures Of Yona Book #4

(Of a Series)

Karen R Olive

The Adventures of Yona Book #4© 2022, Karen Olive, All rights reserved.

INSPIRE OTHERS!
"Please Share These Books!"

For bulk purchases and signed copies contact Karen Olive at KarenROlive@aol.com

This book is Dedicated to:

As my series comes to an end I have to thank the one person to whom I am internally grateful. Without her, there would be no book, no series, and no me, as I know myself today. I'm stronger and more understanding of grief and I have Lori Raupe to thank for that. She shared the butterfly moments of her daughter, our long talks about grief, and how she understood me, even though our world seems so far apart; a California publisher and Polk County small-town girl. Thank you Lori for everything you have made possible for me. I can never repay you for what you have done in front and behind the scenes. God Bless you. My new friend for life.

Also, I want to dedicate this last book to everyone who lost their lives in the horrific Hurricane Ian in September 2022. You will never be forgotten. What sadness for all the people affected by this monster and especially the ones who suffered great loss and devastation. We are so sorry for your loss and pray every day for comfort for you and your families.

I also want to thank all the readers and supporters of "*The Adventures of Yona*" series. Without you, none of this would have been possible. You are and will always be a big part of our lives. You all have become our friends and we are thankful for not only your support but for your friendship as well. I wish I could name each one of you separately but I would be so afraid I would leave one person out, but you all know who you are. Thank you from the bottom of our hearts. I know I sound like a broken record but it bears repeating.

I also want to dedicate this book to my family. My brothers Billy Turner and his wife Erin, Kenneth Turner, and Rocky Jordan. We grew up in an old frame house that we called home. My brothers and I fought as most kids do. But boy when it came to anyone else bothering one of us we banded together protecting each other with no hesitation. Especially when it came to me, being the only girl and all. Billy. Kenneth and Rocky. I love you three with all my heart and I am so so proud to call you my brothers.

Just like you all, we have had a lot of hardship in our lives and just like y'all, we have to keep going. This book has come to an end and I pray that I can move on to my next adventure in life, which is going to feel pretty lonesome. I will feel lost for a while not posting every day. But I have plans, plans to continue on and to live life like I know the ones who have gone on before us, would want us to do. GOD BLESS YOU ALL!

In Praise of The Adventures of Yona

Awesome read about the tales of Yona and a new life in her forever home. I give this book five out of five stars! I enjoyed reading about the daily adventures of Yona! She is so curious about this new world and this book captures all the fun, curious, mischievous, things she does and how she deals with the challenges of being a new pup!
Dawn Elliott

Wouldn't the world be a better place if we could all see it from a dog's point of view? If only we could see everything as a dog sees it I believe this world would not be in the shape it is in today. Karen Olive and her daily posts of Yona have opened up, not only my eyes but the eyes of everyone who follows her.
Yona sees the world as an opportunity to live life to the fullest. She never meets a stranger and she loves everyone. She does have a few struggles along the way. But that's just life. As Yona says in her book. Not everything is going to be perfect all the time. It's how you deal with the situation that matters. Yona is a fun-loving, Mischievous, beautiful Siberian Husky with a lot to say and she will keep you entertained with each page you read. But she will also teach you a few life lessons along the way. If only through the eyes of a dog we could see the beauty and face the world head-on with as positive an attitude as Yona. I believe life would be a whole lot better for us all. Way to go Karen for getting into the heart of a dog and showing us all how wonderful our world is that we live in. It really is up to us how we choose to travel this road of life. I hope you do more books of Yona. I am going to miss reading about her daily adventures.
Molly Sanchez

Since the first time Yona was introduced to us, we fell in love with that cute little innocent face. Each adventure got more interesting as we all watched her grow up. How marvelous it is to hear Yona tell her stories each and every day. That was a way to escape from the everyday life we all have to go through even if only for a few moments. Reading her stories to my grandchildren and seeing them believe that Yona really was telling the story. The true innocence of children as they watch a puppy grow up and how she loves her Mommy and Daddy, and making new friends. Karen is a wonderful author and we are very lucky to be a part of her stories of a precious young dog. Thank you for giving us an escape if only for a short time each day.
Stacee Sherrouse
Polk County School Bus Driver

I have thoroughly enjoyed following the daily adventures of Yona. They have been creative, interesting, and entertaining, and matching the pictures with the storylines has been very enjoyable. I am so proud of you my sweet niece for writing these stories and publishing them. I wish you much success.
Paula Turner Bond

Yona is a beautifully curious Siberian husky with a bright and colorful personality that she just loves to show off! She has the most contagious smile…. Yes, she SMILES! And you just can't read about her without smiling as well! Yona's mom, Karen, shares her journey with us as she grows up and navigates her ever-expanding world. Karen's writing style is captivating and draws you into Yona's energy. Every day with Yona is an adventure; meeting new friends, learning new lessons, and making new memories! Reading about this spunky pup puts a smile on my face every time! Karen and Yona have such good energy together! They truly are a match made in Heaven!
Nevaeh Hailey

The Adventures of Yona is a feel-good, easy read, saga about a sweet little puppy named Yona. Yona takes you through the journeys of her days with a wide-eyed innocent view of the world. To know Yona is to love Yona and once you meet her you will never forget her. Her antics are hysterical and you will laugh out loud. Sit down, take a break, and let Yona show you her world.
Raina Holley

I love the adventures of Yona! The curious nature of Yona is addicting. Her delightful outlook on life is a beautiful example of love and innocence. This book captures the heart of anybody who reads it. Mrs. Olive is an amazing storyteller and you will laugh out loud at Yona's misadventures. A surefire classic in the making.
Kim McCulley

Dogs are a man's "best friend". The Adventures of Yona is a wonderful example of how much a dog can be a friend. Yona makes friends everywhere she goes. This is more than a book about a dog, it is a book about friendship, family, and dog treats. Anyone who meets Yona becomes friends with her instantly. I would recommend this book to anyone!
Uriah Holley

Seeing the world through the eyes of Yona, as written by her mommy Karen Olive, is a refreshing way to remember to take life slow and to appreciate everything that every day brings. Yona figuring out her surroundings even as she is a little bit older now is always entertaining and hearing about her adventures makes my day! Karen beautifully captures the playful essence of growing up, even if it is from a fluffy perspective. Yona's voice shines through and you can't but giggle as you read about her endeavors and how she learns to make sense of the things around her and the connections she makes with new friends, both human and animal! Not to mention how the unconditional love she shows for everyone shows the spirit of our four-legged friends in a true light, as

even when she gets in trouble, Yona wouldn't dare miss the opportunity to get kisses and cuddles.
Elizabeth Perdomo

Karen has a great writing style that really gives the feeling that you are actually hearing what the beautiful curious puppy, Yona is thinking. I would wake up each morning and look for her daily posts for a great laugh and now it's all in one book! A great book for young and old alike!!!
Kimberly

I highly recommend this page for Yona and mommy. Yona has filled my heart again. I was deeply depressed after my Sadie girl passed on July 4th last year. Yona puts a smile on my face every morning.
Her posts are like my morning coffee. don't think my day would start right if I don't read it first thing. I want to keep reading these posts. They make my day smoother and more importantly ease my heartache.
Jessie Melton

In Memory of
Wanda (Joyce) Moses-Flynn
March 26, 1944 - October 8, 2021

Mama was one of the strongest women I have ever met. As a child growing up, I remember she almost always worked two jobs to feed us four kids, put clothes on our backs, and shoes on our feet. I know I mentioned that before, but it bears repeating. She would get up every morning and cook a full breakfast for us kids, before she would go to work, which included homemade biscuits most of the time. Everything she cooked was from scratch. When the microwave came out, she got one. But she hardly ever used it. She was accustomed to cooking off the stove and in the oven. Old habits are hard to break. We always had everything we needed and a lot of what we wanted within reason. Every day after work, she would cook a balanced meal which usually consisted of one meat, potatoes, a vegetable, homemade biscuits, and sweet tea.

Mama had a routine that we all followed. With four kids, organization was very important to her, from the order we got our baths to our chores. We all four had our own chores, and not doing them was not an option, we were dusting, vacuuming, sweeping, mopping, and cleaning the bathrooms. Mama usually washed and folded all the clothes and bleached the kitchen down, them were just the Saturday chores. All five of us, including Mama, had our daily chores to do also, and we did them before we went and played. We took turns each week washing the dishes, I think Billy had the trash duty, and Kenneth and Rocky had to pull weeds in the flower beds, and I helped cook. Our house wasn't much, but it was clean.

One of my fondest memories was Mama teaching me how to make homemade biscuits. Just the two of us bonding over a big Tupperware bowl of flour, buttermilk, and Crisco, and whatever other little ingredients she may have added.

As long as our report cards were good, we would go to the drive-in movies. Mama would make hotdogs and wrap them in aluminum foil, and during the movie, we would eat our hotdogs. I remember them being the best hotdogs I ever had. Hotdogs and grape Kool-Aid. It didn't get any better than that.

Another fond memory was sitting on the porch swing while it was raining. Mama and us four kids would count "one Mississippi" or "one, one-thousand" every time lightning would strike. If the thunder would come before the first count was finished, we would all go inside because Mama said the lightning was less than a mile away. I don't know if that's really true or not, but we believed her. Mama was firm but loving. She had to be, and you better believe we listened. We didn't get cars for our sixteenth birthday, but you better bet we got a homemade cake every single year and a present to open. We all looked forward to her making the birthday cakes because we all got to clean up the cake batter after Mama was done! We took care of all the utensils and the bowl! We enjoyed that a lot.

"We would all enjoy a special birthday meal, then sing "Happy Birthday," and afterwards the birthday girl or boy would blow out the candles. From year to year, another candle was added, another wish, and we blew out the candles with one breath, which grew harder and harder with the growing number of candles! Of course, Mama would give us our birthday "lickin's" with her hand on our bottom side, with, one to grow on, and we would all laugh.

I don't remember if anyone ever got Mama a cake or not. I'm sure as we got older, we made her one. There was a lot of sacrificing on Mama's end to make sure we kids had what we needed. Too bad it wasn't until we were all adults till we understood just how much she sacrificed for us. 'Til this day, I still carry on Mama's tradition of everyone getting a cake on their birthday.

We were not rich by no means. We didn't have central heat and air. But Mama made sure we had the appropriate clothes to wear, and we all got dressed by the old gas heater in the living room on cold winter mornings. We all sat in the living room together each night and watched tv til it was time to go to bed. When bedtime came around, you knew to get up and kiss Mama goodnight and go to bed.

When I became an adult with grown kids of my own. My mama and I had become best friends. We traveled a lot together, the four of us. Mama, her husband (my stepfather) Bob, my husband Roy and me. Them are memories I will cherish for the rest of my life.

We talked on the phone every night. We had the best time planning trips together. I remember when my Mama fell off the ladder and shattered her knee in several places, but I didn't know that it would mark the end of her traveling days.

Then her husband, whom we all loved so dearly, Robert (Bob) Flynn, our stepfather, passed away unexpectedly on December 13th, 2014. She got up that morning and found him in the front bedroom, where he liked to get up in the wee hours and look out from their home's bay window. He was a gentle man, and he always had a smile on his face. Bob was one of the good ones. He never had a bad word to say about anyone. He loved my mama, cherished her, and treated her like a Princess. She actually put a plaque out at the graveside that read, "My husband, Bob, was my Prince."

My mama never got over losing Bob. It turned out to be the downfall of the mama we had once known. I would call her and say, " I need my mama!" She would say, "I'm right here." But the truth was she wasn't. Not the one I knew anyway. She came to live with Roy and me in May of 2021.

Little did we know we wouldn't have her long. She passed away on October 8th, 2021, leaving many unanswered questions and "why" behind.

Before my mama fell off the ladder and shattered her knee, I will never forget her saying, "Karen, if I could take a trip to Alaska, I would die a happy woman." Well, Mama got her wish! To honor her I felt it was appropriate to add these family photos and some of our trip to Alaska with Bob and Roy.

I love and miss Mama more than anyone will ever know. I feel as though if I stop writing, her memories will fade away. And I also love and miss Bob with all my heart. There is much more to say, but I must stop somewhere. "Til we meet again, Mama. You took a piece of my heart when you left. But it's not 'goodbye' it's, I'll see you soon in God's time."

In Memory of
Gregory Daniel Olive
December 13, 1966 - June 6, 2021

Greg married Tammy Ann Olive on September 6th, 1986, at Bethel Baptist Church in Lakeland, Florida. They had one child, Matthew Olive, born at Titusville Hospital on June 6th, 1994

Greg loved his toys; motorcycles, dirt bikes, MG cars, and boats! He was a big Miami Dolphins' fan. He even dressed to the occasion for every game. He would jump up and cheer for his team like no other. Roy was so proud of him. The things Greg had stored in that brain of his was nothing short of miraculous, mind-boggling, really. The same respect Roy had for his son, Greg had for his dad. Picking his dad's brain was one of his favorite past times. They had a special bond, just like Greg had with his son Matthew.

Greg served in the Air Force at Eglin Airforce Base in Fort Walton Beach, Florida, from 1986-1990. Greg knew from a young age what he wanted to do, and soon, his dreams would become a reality. His passion was working at the Kennedy Space Center. He was a Shuttle Technician for the space shuttle program and then on the Orion program. Greg was part of "The Pad Rats," and he proudly wore that title with his coworkers.

Greg loved to talk and wasn't afraid of a friendly debate. He would defend his opinion 'til the end. But if, by chance, someone could prove him wrong. He conceded with grace and made sure to let the other person know what a good point they made. He was full of knowledge and really enjoyed talking to anyone, no matter what the topic was.

Greg was a big family man. His family is what he lived for, Tammy and Matthew. Everything he was building was for them, as they would soon find out.

On June 14th, 2019, Greg was diagnosed with stage four lung cancer and was given about three years to live. He was so courageous, given his diagnosis. And like everyone would and should, he got a second opinion, which would not turn out to be in his favor. The time he thought he had was considerably shorter than initially told. Greg now had to break this news to his family. Greg seemed to be in total control, trying to console his family with the bad news he dreaded sharing. I'm sure he had moments of despair, but he never dwelled on the negative for too long. He took what life had to throw at him head-on. He knew the next Christmas would probably be his last, not that he was giving up hope. But he knew in his heart that time was drawing near, so he was very persistent in taking lots of pictures that Christmas, and that's exactly what we did.

Despite everything, he always tried to keep a smile on his and his family's faces. He was always putting everyone else's needs before his own and made daily life as normal as possible. He didn't want fanfare, people making a fuss, or pity. He just wanted to get on with his life with what time was left and live it to its fullest. His main goal with the time he had left was to ensure his family was taken care of, paying off all the bills, including the house. He did not want to leave his wife, Tammy, with any big bills to deal with.

He made sure his son Matthew had everything he needed to start his own life. Matthew really didn't need any help in that respect, but Greg wanted to be a part of it. Even if he wasn't there to see it. Matthew focused all of his energy on being there for his dad. He even started working from home just to be close to him and help him in any way he could. Even though Greg didn't want Matthew to put his life on hold for him, I know he really appreciated it, and the extra time he could spend with his son would be good for them both. I believe Greg knew Matthew needed to do this. Not only for Greg but for himself also.

Greg called me one day while I was working to ask me a question about his dad. As we were hanging up, Greg said, "Hey Karen, you're going to miss me when I'm gone." Truer words were never spoken.

Greg passed away on Matthew's birthday. No one really knows. But the word WHY always seems to come to mind at times like this. It wasn't meant for us to know or ask why. His coworkers posted a picture with all their Miami Dolphins jerseys on. The caption simply stated, "Godspeed, Greg Olive."

Goodbyes are not forever. Goodbyes do not mean the end. They simply mean I'll miss you until we meet again.

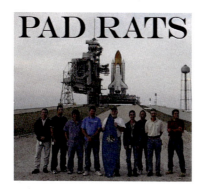

Forward

It is so hard to believe *The Adventures of Yona - Book #4,* and this four-book series is finished. What a wild ride! This experience will be in my memories for as long as I live. It has been so special to get to know Karen and to see her passion for bringing Yona to all of you. It has been wonderful to encourage her to help her walk out of her comfort zone and right into a new version of herself. It has been so rewarding and quite fun all at the same time to be a part of this project.

However, Karen has pushed through a myriad of emotions to get these books done for you. The impetus to continue when it wasn't easy for her was powered by grief, which I saw turn into love for all of you. It has been difficult at times, as I have seen Karen's grief which is real and raw. I am so grateful to have been able to be an understanding friend in some of her difficult moments.

Karen is the definition of perseverance. In September, we saw Hurricane Ian travel through Florida. Leaving a path of destruction, at the last minute it headed right through Polk County, where Karen and many of her family members live. I stayed up all night praying because I couldn't imagine Karen going through any more heartache. Gratefully they were all spared devastation. But many people continue to suffer with the loss of everything they have known and try to rebuild their lives. Having experienced the loss of my home in the past, my heart breaks as I see what Hurricane Ian caused.

One of my dreams has come to pass also thanks to Karen's willingness to let them help us. In 2014, I wrote in my journal that I wanted my family to join me in business. I could never have imagined how this heart's desire would play out. Recently, my granddaughters started helping me in this business with editing and video book trailers. Dreams do come true.

In this book, Yona continues to share her life experiences of family, friends, and even hardship. Thank you for being an encourager and for taking the time to read these books. You are appreciated beyond measure by both Karen and me.

A giant "thank you" to Karen for sharing this experience with me. And an equally enormous "thank you" to you for encouraging Karen, and loving Yona as you do. Yona is no longer a puppy and, spoiler alert, she turns one year old and celebrates with those she loves. It is our hope that you see life a little brighter, and feel more joy and happiness as you go on the adventures with Yona.

Every day is a gift, there is a beautiful world around us to explore if we just look around. We have the opportunity to share Yona with those you know and care about, so please tell people about these books. So many people have fear for the future, they need hope, a little laughter, and to escape for a little while. What better way than to do it through Yona's eyes? Surly Yona is the one who will be up for the challenge to bring hope to those you love!

Thank you again, Karen, for allowing me to be a part of your life, and share Yona with the world.

Lori Raupe
The Butterfly Publishing Company

A Note For You

We all knew this time would come, but it's so bittersweet because I feel like I have accomplished something that will be here for generations. From my friends and family down to their kids and grandkids, and for that, I am happy and grateful. It also feels like I am saying "goodbye" to the reason I wrote this little series to begin with, and that saddens me greatly.

I will never forget all the encouraging words from each and every one of you. It amazed me how everyone came together and joined in to help me with this series. Knowing we all probably have at least one thing in common... that's grief! The loss of a loved one. I always said if you live long enough, you are going to feel heartache. I didn't know the impact it would have. I didn't realize how powerful grief could be. I didn't know how debilitating it really was. With the help of Yona and all of you, I have managed to survive this horrific ordeal. I'm not out of the woods yet. Heck, I may never be the same again. I guess I'm not really expected to be, am I? None of us are. But we also know life has to go on. That, for me, was the hardest part...life going on. I have good days, and I have bad days. My bad days are really bad. But, they are getting fewer and farther between. Not a lot, but not as bad as it was. We continue to redirect and try to hold on to the happy memories we have made. But sometimes it's just too unbearable to deal with, and we have a "bad day" Does it hurt just as bad today as the day they both left? Absolutely! Can I go a day without thinking about them? No. Can I go for a day without crying? Yes, I can. But when it comes, it comes, and not much can stop it. You never know what day or time it will hit. When it does, it hits with a vengeance. I will be lost for a while, I think. But hopefully, we will be able to move on to our next adventure. My husband and I need to find ourselves. What I mean by that is it's time for us now. We need to find some normalcy in this crazy uncertain world we live in today. It's a new chapter in our lives. To go on without the ones we love.

Nonetheless, we have to continue. God is in control. It's not up to us to ask why? It's our job to trust Him and continue on until he calls us home. You all, along with my family, have been my rock, and I love you for that. Thank you from the bottom of my heart. You were all there when I needed someone most. There is a lot of you, and I didn't ever feel alone. I can't begin to tell you all just how much I appreciate each and every one of you! God Bless You All!!!

Love,
Karen Olive

The Teeny Weeny Doggie Door

Hello, my friends, it's nice to be back and to talk to you again. I would like to draw your attention to this so-called "doggie door" behind me. Take a good look at me and then take another look at that teeny weeny doggie door. Now, what am I supposed to do with that? My Green bone could hardly fit through there. Evidently, I am their first big dog that's ever been allowed in the house because I know that door was not put in for me. If it was, Mama and Daddy underestimated the growth of a husky. I'm a little over 9 1/2 months old and I may not be done growing yet. Mama put the slider on it to keep me from getting my head stuck through it. That's a scary thought. I suppose the last doggie they had was a small doggie. Now that I think about it. I have heard them talk about a little Pomeranian named Mandi. I bet that was her doggie door. I bet if she were still here today we would be best friends. I'm sad I never got to meet her. She sounded like she would have been fun to play with, even though I did hear she could be a little bossy at times. But anyways. I wonder what Mama and Daddy is going to do about this doggie door. Anyone have a measuring tape?

Mama Come Look At The Birdie

Mama, look at the birdie. It's just standing there by the water's edge. It's not scared of any alligator or snake or me even! I wonder what it's doing? Do you think it wants to come over here and play with me? I wonder if it's a boy or a girl. Hey birdie, are you a boy or a girl? What's your name? Do you want to come play in my playground? We can play chase but you have to run and not fly. It would be cheating if you fly because then I couldn't catch you because I don't know how to fly. Hey, birdie can you hear me?

Mama, that birdie is not paying me one bit of attention. Either that, or it forgot its hearing aids like Daddy does sometimes. Well. Okay birdie, I hope you don't get ate by an alligator standing that close to the water. That's why my daddy built me a fence so I could run inside before the alligator got over the fence because I can run really fast. Do you want to see?

Hey, birdie? Mama, I think that birdie might be shy. Let's just continue playing fetch with my green bone. If the birdie sees how much fun we are having, maybe it will join us. Okay, Mama? Hey birdie, watch this?

I Can't Wait To Show My Daddy

Oh boy, oh boy, oh boy, I am so excited! I can't wait to show my daddy what I got! Me and my daddy get up every morning and have daddy-daughter time while my mama gets a few extra minutes of beauty sleep. That's funny...beauty sleep. But anyways, after my daddy pets me for a long time, he lets me go out and explore my playground all by myself, without someone constantly telling me to come in. Daddy says I am a big girl now.

But anyways, I worked really hard chewing on this two-foot black root, and I finally got it. I went running into the house, and I ran right between my daddy's legs with my black root flapping in the wind and dropped it right at his feet. About that time, my daddy jerked his legs up really high and then started stomping on my root like nothing I have ever seen before! Daddy! What are you doing to my root? Poor root!

Later, after Mama got up, I heard Daddy telling Mama he thought I brought him a snake. Well, at least he didn't scream like a girl like Mama did when she thought I brought her a snake. What is it with them and snakes anyways? I wish I had a video camera. I would have got a great video of my daddy. If I knew how to use one that is. Hey Daddy, I didn't know you could move that fast.

Miracles happen every day, change your perception of what a miracle is and you'll see them all around you.

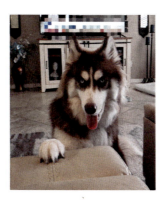

I'm Telling Mama!

I found a new chew toy by the little fishies' pond and it was just the right size to fit in my mouth. But when I tried to bring it into the house, my daddy met me at the door and took it away from me! I was getting pretty use to Mama taking things away from me. Now my daddy! I don't know how to break this to you Daddy, but I'm only almost ten months old. Me putting things in my mouth is not going to stop anytime soon... This will not be the last time we run into a situation like this. It may be best for you to look the other way, 'cause I'm going to be doing this a lot and I'm faster than you. Besides, taking things out of my mouth is Mama's job.

Speaking of Mama, I'm telling on you! Mama, Mama, Daddy took my chew toy out of my mouth without my permission. No means no! What do you mean you're on Daddy's side? Oh boy, this is going to be a long rebellious teenage phase. Thanks for having my back on this Mama! Not! Whatever happened to man's best friend?

Is That For Me?

Hey Mama, whatcha doing over there? Is that for me? Do you need any help? I'm a big help. I can…well, I can… hmmm, I know I can do something to help. If you tell me what you're doing, I'm sure I can figure out something to do. I know, you make something and I will taste it for you. I'll see if it's any good. I know I can do that! Whatcha making anyways? A cake, rotisserie chicken, hot dogs?

You're making what? You're making me dog food! What's in it? Cake, rotisserie chicken, hot dogs? What? Rice, ground turkey, and vegetables?!? Well, I guess I could try it. It sounds kinda good. You know I will try anything once. Maybe twice if I like it. Who knows? Just fix me a bowl and I'll let you know if I like it or not. But don't be too disappointed if I don't like it. I mean, without rotisserie chicken or hot dogs, it's going to be questionable but you might get lucky. But if you promise to give me a doggie ice cream afterwards. I will try my best to act like I like it. Even if I don't. But don't forget the doggie ice cream.

My Daddy's Human Son Greg

My daddy told me a story about his human son Greg, he had a very important job. He worked on the space shuttles! My Daddy said Greg was a very smart man. He loved his family so much and he was loved by everybody. I did not get to meet him, but I wish I had. He sounds like a very interesting man. I bet he would have really liked me. Tammy was his wife and she is one of the nicest people I have ever met. I can't wait to go see her and Greg's son Matthew this week. They are my family too.

The exciting part is that Matthew gets to pick up from where his daddy left off on working on getting humans back to the moon with NASA's Artemis. Matthew gets to work alongside his daddy's friends and coworkers from the space shuttle and carry on the journey and legacy. Why? Because he now works where his daddy did!

What an amazing story. Greg, Tammy and Matthew were a very tight-knit family and I know Tammy and Matthew miss Greg terribly. I know my daddy and Mama sure do too!. I know he has to be looking down at Matthew with a big smile on his face because he is so proud of him. Way to Go Matthew! I will see you soon. Road Trip!

GREG [LEFT] AND MATTHEW [RIGHT]

My Mama Went Night Swimming

Hey Mama, what are you doing in that cement pond all by yourself at dark time? Did someone throw you in? Do you need me to help you get out? What? You got in all by yourself and you are not even scared? No, no, no. You can try as hard as you want to get me to come in with you but the answer will still be the same. It's not happening. It does seem pretty and bright but it's also wet and deep! So it will be a 'NO' from me Mama. Sorry but I am not ready for all that wetness, plus it messes up my hair. I will just stay right here and watch you swim. You have fun, and one day, maybe when I am one year old, I might get in there with you.

For now, I will just go get you a towel and stand here and wait for you. What do you mean no? Well, I guess you're right, I would take the towel out in my playground and shred it into little pieces and eat it. But what do you expect? I'm a doggie! I guess Daddy will have to get a towel for you. Besides, I'm tired of standing here watching you swim. It's kinda boring. I'll be out plundering around in my playground if anyone wants me. That's what doggies do. We like to night plunder. We can find all kinds of interesting things if we look hard enough. I'll be back. She's all yours, Daddy, don't forget the towel.

Going Visiting

Oh boy, oh boy, oh boy, it's road trip time! We are headed to see my other family. Tammy, Matthew, and Ellie. Let's not forget their fur doggies, Lita and Fender. I'm sooo happy! We are going to have sooo much fun! We are going to play chase all over the house. We are going to eat doggie ice cream and play tug-of-war. I brought treats for everybody! We are going to go outside and explore their playground. I'm so excited! There is no telling what treasures I'm going to find. It's going to be the best time ever!

Can anyone say, slumber party doggie style! Woohoo! So five minutes into the car ride I ask, "Are we there yet?" Another five minutes goes by, and I ask, "Are we there yet?" This went on and on and on for about two hours until I was like, "I don't even care anymore!" Then, finally!!! Just as I was about to give up, we pulled into my family's driveway. I forgot how long that car ride was. I really don't enjoy that part at all! Thank goodness we finally made it. It's party time! Look out, family, here I come!

Snack Time

I've had the best time ever! Lita, Fender, and I have worn each other out playing so hard. Lita and Fender are older than me but I can still run as fast as they can because I'm really really fast. I just wish they lived closer so we could see each other more often. You know, because I don't like long car rides and all. But, it was all worth it once we got here.

We have played every game you could imagine. I have chewed and squeaked every toy in their toy box. Lita and Fender have a lot of toys! Way more than me, because, well, I tear my toys up. But it's not my fault. I'm an aggressive chewer. That's what they say anyway. Why, it only took me five minutes to tear the ear off of one of their toys. Tammy said it was a very strong toy, and she didn't think I could break it. Well, I did! Sorry, Tammy, Lita, and Fender.

After we played and played and played, we all three settled down for a yummy doggie treat. I have had the best time and I cannot wait to do this again. I will probably sleep for two days when I get home. I'm sure Mama and Daddy will too. You can't ever have too much fun. So they say anyway. So, who is going to clean up all this mess?

Ten Months Old Today

Another month older today, can you believe it? Ten months old, double digits, almost grown. You won't believe what I got for my tenth-month birthday! I would show it to you but it hasn't got here yet! Mama ordered me one of those loud piggy chewy toys of my very own and boy, oh boy, I can't wait 'til it gets here. I'm sure my daddy is not very pleased with my mama for buying it. But, he will get over it. Just take your hearing aids out Daddy, it will be okay. I sure hope it is as sturdy as they say it is. I want to keep it for a very long time. It sounds just like a real piggy, so I've heard.

You remember I played with one at my family's house. I also got a bone chewy toy. They say it tastes like beef. Yummy! We will see. The delivery man should be here sometime today. My daddy went and bought me this chew toy that has a ball in it to pacify me until my other toys arrive. I really love it too. Except for this ball inside of it is too big to come out of the holes. I have been trying to get it out all morning long! I bet they did this on purpose. But I'm going to keep working on it because I'm pretty good at figuring these things out. Maybe that's why Mama and Daddy said I can only play with it while they are around. Safety first you know. Daddy, where is that delivery man? Doesn't he know it's my birthday?

No matter how rough the road may be,

we can and we will, never, never...

... never give up on our dreams!

Here Piggy Piggy

Seriously, the best thing ever! My piggy chew toy. I wish you could hear it. It sounds just like a piggy. Even though I have never seen or heard a real piggy make a noise. My daddy said he has, and it sounds just like one. I could chew on this all day long but it seems to disappear for about two hours at a time. I'm not naming any names but I do see this guilty look on my daddy's face and he does sit right in front of his ottoman. We all know that's where my toys go to sleep. Some for a very, very, very long time. Then, when I least expect it. My piggy just reappears from out of nowhere. It has already disappeared about five times and I just got it yesterday!

But when I do have it, I make it squeak, squeak, squeak all over the house. Especially, by my daddy's chair. I thought my daddy was hard of hearing but he said nobody is that hard of hearing. I think my daddy was putting a spin on his words. My mama said I better watch my piggy very closely because before you know it. My daddy will be taking my little piggy to the market! Mama, what's a market?

Poor Piggy Piggy

Well, my daddy will not have to worry about taking my piggy to the market, whatever that means. I was chewing and making it squeal as loud as I could when suddenly before I knew it, I was chewing on my poor piggy's leg! And it wasn't even attached to my piggy! Mama, with her peripheral vision, caught me as I was swallowing it down. My poor piggy's leg didn't stand a chance.

Needless to say, my piggy went straight in the garbage because I saw Mama put it in there. All the while, I was jumping up at her showing my dislike of her unfair decision-making. It was just a leg! Piggy had three more! Mama said I was lucky it was a little leg and she didn't see where I would have any issues passing it. Yuk, Mama! Kids are reading this! But anyways, Mama said she wasn't going to give me the chance to eat the other three legs. I'm offended that she even said that.

Poor piggy, I guess she would have been better off with Daddy. At least she would have got to go shopping at the market. Mean Mama. Oh well, at least I still have my bone.

Happy Birthday to me! Yummy bone. Bye, little Piggy. Mama said safety first, Yona, that's me, Yona. Live and learn, live and learn.

Live to learn,

and you will really learn to live!

My Daddy's Birthday

Yesterday was Daddy's birthday! Only two days after mine. But his is in years! Mine is still in months. We had a late birthday party for my daddy. My older big sister, Kari, and her boyfriend-fiance came over. My youngest big sister, Kara, and her boyfriend came over too. Guess who else came over? You guessed it! My Littles came!

My daddy was so happy. We had a lot of food and cake and ice cream! They all sang, "Happy Birthday to Daddy," and I helped! Then Mama cut the cake. I didn't get any cake but I did get some of my doggie ice cream. See, Mama and Daddy are very good at including me in all the family functions. That makes me feel good.

But anyways, back to Daddy. I think he really enjoyed his birthday. Especially all that food! My daddy loves to eat as much as I do. Especially cake and ice cream. He got presents too. I'm glad my daddy had a good birthday because he works very hard and he deserves it. Happy Birthday Daddy, I love you! So, what's the chance that I can get some cake to go with this ice cream?

Mama's Favorite Shoe

So, I may have chewed my mama's favorite shoe. I only chewed it a little but evidently, I chewed it in a very noticeable spot. Like right on top! It gets worse. The shoe I chewed on was the shoes my mama got from her mama! Oh boy, I think I really hurt my mama by doing that. She wore them all the time. But now one has a big chew spot on top. I did hear my mama say it was her fault because she left them on the floor. But actually, she put them right beside her, by the couch on the floor, to keep an eye on them. But I saw them and I snuck one while she wasn't looking. Mama even brought me my food to eat in the living room because I wouldn't get up and go eat it. She put it on a paper plate and everything. But instead, I went over to my daddy's ottoman and hid behind it, and chewed my mama's shoe. I feel really bad, but that is what doggies do though. They chew things. I just wish it hadn't been Mama's favorite shoes that came from her mama. She is so sentimental about things like that. I have to try and make it up to her somehow. But I don't know how. I am sure I will think of something. I just hope it will be enough. I hope she knows how sorry I am. I knew better too; that's why I hid and chewed it. I just couldn't help myself. I'm sorry Mama, can you ever forgive me? You can have my food if you want.

I Ate My Harness

I have a very important day today and Mama has planned everything to a tee. Tables, chairs; the whole setup has been planned. I have been to the groomers and had my hair done. I went to Little Wolfe's Pet Resort in Winter Haven. That place is awesome. The owner was there and she was very nice. She said we could say the name of her business in our book.

But anyways, Mama had my leash and harness all laid out for me to use for today. Well, I kinda reached up there on the high bar outside and took the harness out into my wet muddy playground, while mama was out having her hair done. Daddy was supposed to be watching me. Boy, oh boy, I bet daddy is in trouble. He is not a very good doggie watcher.

But anyways, I ate my harness. That's two I have done like that, so far. Mama better keep her day job 'cause I'm starting to get expensive. Between toys, food, groomers and now these harnesses. So now I have to go to my event with my collar and leash. Daddy said the other harness will not be here in time. He also said it's my fault that I have to wear the collar.

Well, the way I see it, Mama and Daddy both know I'm getting bigger. I'm a curious doggie so why was the harness left unattended and within my reach? Hey, Where is my daddy anyways, because when Mama gets home and sees me all dirty like this right before our big event in a few hours somebody is going to be in T-R-O-U-B-L-E!!!

Choose to take responsibility for your life, you will immediately gain an increased capacity to achieve your greatest potential.

Meet And Great

Oh, what a day I had yesterday! I met so many people. They were so nice! They all petted me, and I had treats left and right. I had my picture taken with most everyone who came. People bought my books and played with me. I even got gifts!! I just can't tell you how excited I was. Well, maybe I can. I was good almost all of the time. I did try to eat my leash a few times. Oh, who am I kidding? I tried my best to chew it in half. But each person that came in would redirect me, and I would stop. For a little while, anyways. I think people really like me. But what's not to like, right?

Except maybe chewing up everything I get my teeth on. But other than that, I'm a good girl. I'm going to dedicate a page to everyone who came out to see me and my mama!. It was really nice to meet some of the people who read the posts about me on Facebook and who took the time out of their busy schedules just to come out and meet me.

It makes me all warm and fuzzy inside. Or, maybe it was the big treat that did that. Either way, it felt good. I want you all to know I had a great time, and so did Mama. When I got home, I ate, went outside for a minute, and then slept for the rest of the day and night. Having fun is exhausting.

Thank you all, and I hope to see you all again soon. And a big shout out to PGF Nutrition for letting us have our event at your establishment. It was so nice of you to welcome us like you did. Thank you Miss Tammy and Miss Vanessa for helping Mama with our big day. You all are the best friends ever! Thank you!

We All Knew It

I was laying there in my nice cozy bed when I thought to myself, *Yona, there is a little wrinkle in your bed.* So, I took it upon myself to straighten up my bed. I pushed the wrinkle with my nose and it just came back. I pushed it the other way with my nose and the same thing happened. So I grabbed it with my teeth and oops! Well, the wrinkle went away but... Woohoo!!!! What a hidden treasure I found inside. Boy, oh boy, this is fun. The more I ripped the more treasure I found. Nice soft foam that I could rip so easily with my teeth. It was like a foam party in my cage.

One rip, two rips, three rips, four! Seriously, I haven't had this much fun in a long time. Just me all by myself. Me and my bed. Pure pleasure of ripping and tearing and... I can't even stand it. I'm having so much fun. Oh no, someone's coming! I can't get the foam back in the bed fast enough.

Okay Mama, here is my defense. We all knew it was just a matter of time before I was going to do this. I can't believe you really seem surprised by it. Why are you acting like it wasn't going to happen? You know I have been tearing up and eating everything I get my mouth on. So really, you shouldn't be surprised at all. I'm just a doggie you know. Green really wasn't my color anyways. When you order another one, can you get it in light blue to match my eyes? If you don't mind, order it for next-day shipping because this cage bottom is hard. What?

Pull Rope Mishap

I was playing with my pull rope, Mama, and Daddy got me. You know, the one that hangs on the tree outside? I was having so much fun 'til all of a sudden, the rope went around my bottom jaw. My mama was sitting on the patio and she was keeping an eye on me but she couldn't see the rope caught around my jaw. I finally just stood still and that got my mama's attention because I am never still. She started walking closer and closer to me until she finally saw the rope around my bottom jaw. My mama worked and worked trying to get it loose because it was very very tight.

Finally, she kept twisting the rope around and around until it got loose enough for me to get my jaw out. That was not very fun and I don't think I will play with that anymore. Not today anyways. After I got free I went into the house and took a long nap. Thank you Mama for helping me. Mean old rope! The more I tugged the tighter it got. It's a good thing Mama keeps a good eye on me. But, one could also argue, if she had been keeping a better eye on me, it wouldn't have happened in the first place, just saying. I love you, Mama.

A Storm's A-Brewin'

Everybody's busy, busy, busy around here. My Daddy, Uncle Rocky, and Harry are boarding up and battening down the hatches. Mama said we're gonna have to hunker down. I hunker down every day so that will not be hard for me. Mama's been in the kitchen cooking up a storm. No pun intended. The rains here and we got a lot to do before Hurricane Ian comes through. Everything has to come in. There's no time to waste. Everyone seems to know what to do because they have been through this before so I guess I will be safe in their hands.

My Littles are already here and there will be more joining us later. I don't really know what all to expect but I'm going to go with the flow. If ever I needed to mind Mama and Daddy it looks like now is the time. I just want to know one thing. Where am I supposed to go after I eat? You all know what I mean. If it's raining real hard I can't go outside and I have no idea how to use one of those white bowls that Lita drinks out of. I followed someone in there one time but I don't think I can do that. What if I fall in? I don't think y'all know the stress we animals go through during times like these. I am going to try not to think about it. I hope you all stay safe and listen to your fur babies. When they let you know they gotta go and they most likely will. You better have a plan or it won't be pretty! That's all I'm going to say. Stay safe my friends.

There are no "secrets" to success.

It is the result of preparation, hard work, and learning from failure.

Hurricane Ian - Sept. 28th, 2022

I don't know why, but I just keep on and on, getting in trouble. First of all I wouldn't stay off my Littles. Then I went outside and got sidetracked by a huge palm tree limb. Well, I sure was having fun with that limb. Mama tried to get me to come in, but nope, I wasn't coming in. The rain was just pouring down, and I was having a ball. Mama was soaked before it was all over. My oldest big sister Kari tried to get me to come in and I ran the other way. Limbs were flying everywhere! Woohoo!

Then Daddy came to get me! No more foolin' around 'cause he means business. Then they dried me off and I rested for a while, but I wanted out again! But this time, Mama put that mean ol' leash on me and made me go out with it on. I kept jumping on her and pulling and tugging. Showing my dislike as much as possible.

Mama was getting wet and when I tell you she went from Mama to some kind of scary she monster after I jumped on her for the third time! She grabbed me and brought me inside and I had to sit in my doggie crate for two hours and think about how I should have behaved. I'm going to have nightmares about that face and the look in her eyes. She really shouldn't stress me out like that. They should give me a break cause this was my first hurricane you know. I can't help it if I enjoyed playing fetch with the flying tree limbs. Now I'm gonna be seeing my trainer sooner than later, I'm afraid. But, it wasn't all bad though. I still have my Littles. Kayle, could you scratch a little more to the left?

This ain't no party, this ain't no disco,
I'm tellin' ya, this ain't no fooling around.

Daddy Call The Coast Guard

I have been watching a lot of TV, and if there is one thing I have learned...where water is involved, you call the Coast Guard. They need to come and get this water out of my playground. I mean, one minute I was chewing on roots, and the next minute we need a boat! I know my playground is under there somewhere. I just hope there are not any of them stinky floppy fishies in there. I don't like those slippery, slimy things.

Daddy, what are you waiting for? Go call them and tell them to come and get their lake. How am I supposed to play in this? But you need to go get some salt first and pour in it cause all the movies I've seen, where the Coast Guard was involved it was always in salt water. So, you're saying they do lakes too? Then go call them. Hurry! This is an emergency! I only have a small area to go out in and you know what I mean by that and I am a big doggie. So it's either, give me more space, or someone needs to grab a baggie.

Mama grabs the baggies all the time. But besides that, I am a runner, not a swimmer. Not to mention this lake is dirty and I can't see the bottom. You know I don't like it when I can't see the bottom. I won't even swim in the cement pond and I can see the bottom of it. Daddy, are you listening to me? I can see this is going nowhere. Hey Mama, come here. Can you call the Coast Guard?

Asking for help is never a sign of weakness.

It's one of the bravest things you can do.

And it can save your life!

Take A Look At This?

Has anyone seen the cement pond? Daddy, I think that underwater submarine thing needs to come and eat all this stuff. The screens are ripped out and all this stuff flew in here. It's kinda hard with no electricity because the generator can only do so much. Oh yeah, did I mention that part? No electricity! Probably we'll be without it for a week, they say. Mama and Daddy have to call and ask people what is going on or drive into town. We don't have any internet right now either, so much for Mama's Google.

My Oldest Big Sister Kari, Youngest Big Sister Kara, the Littles, Matthew and Tammy, and all the rest of Mama and Daddy's families and homes are okay. As a matter of fact, I think everyone they know is okay after that nasty hurricane came and turned my playground into a lake with creepy crawlers in it. My prayers go out to anyone affected by this monster.

Mama and Daddy have two places they have to clean up and they are working very hard. So it's my job to walk around and assess the situation at our house and let them know what all needs to be done.

But anyways, I hope that underwater submarine is hungry! It has a lot of eating to do. Now that I have assessed the cement pond situation, I need to check out the roof. Well, on second thought, that sounds like a job for my daddy. Daddy, the roof is all yours, But I'll help you get the ladder.

Luck can run out...

...but safety is good for life.

I Got Out

So, no one knows exactly how it happened but I got out of my house and into unfamiliar territory. (Daddy left the gate open, "Shhh, don't tell Mama!"). I was just wondering around minding my own business being very mindful to stay close to the house. But let me just say, I had plenty of places I could have gone to at this point. It was an open road to anywhere I wanted to go. But I didn't. I was just plundering around outside. Boy, oh boy, after the hurricane was there a lot of stuff to plunder in! But I did get to see my old friend Brady and Miss Charlotte while I was out.

Then all of a sudden, the doors slammed wide open! Daddy was whistling, Mama had my leash, my bacon treats, and her car keys. I thought to myself, *"Yona."* That's me Yona. *"Yona, what in the world are they doing?"*

Whatever it is, it looks chaotic, but I want to do it too. So I hurried to the back screened door and said. Hey, Mama let me in the screen door so I can do what you two are doing; as soon as I figure out what it is.

By the way, why do you have my leash and bacon treats? Where are you going in such a hurry? Mama was at a fast trot on the way to her car when suddenly she stopped dead in her tracts. Turned around and saw me standing there. Mama and her peripheral vision again. Mama said, "Yona! Come in!" She opened the door and she hugged me really tight. Then started yelling for Daddy who was whistling down the road. I never did find out what all the fuss was about. Come to think about it, I never got one of them doggie bacon treats either. Hey Mama, where's my treat!?!

I Made Mud Pies

Mama, come look! I made you and Daddy a mud pie and they are sooo good. I ate two already. What!?! Why do you have that crazy look in your eyes? What do you mean, "Get off the rug! Get out of the house?" Really? I made you breakfast and I worked hard at it too! And this is the thanks I get. What do you mean don't touch you? Are you being serious right now? This is not my fault. I can't help it that my playground flooded and now it has muddy spots in it everywhere. Everybody knows that rain makes mud and boy did we have rain and well, as you can see, the rest is history.

What do you mean, *my face tells it all*. Let me look in the mirror. I will decide what my face is saying. Although I'm pretty sure a face cannot really talk. I'll look anyway. Oh my, how did all that get on there? Okay, okay, you get the towel and I'll go to the water hose. I know this routine by now. Daddy, seeings you are the one who let me out, you should clean the floor and vacuum the rug. Mama and I are going to get this mud off me. This will be the last time I ever offer you two breakfast again. I'll eat all the mud pies by myself from now on. Mama hurry, my face is starting to dry and crack.

You See This Hat?

This here is my daddy's hat. Now, my daddy knows I have this small problem of chewing on anything and everything I can get my teeth around. So, I ask you, *Why would he leave his hat within my reach?* He knows I lay on the couch now. Yet, here it is...it's like, he is just asking me to take it and chew on it. Like he is just giving it to me really. I keep looking at it and I have seriously thought about it. Like how much fun it would be to chew it up!

But I know Daddy would be very disappointed in me. Kinda like Mama was when I chewed on the shoe her mama gave her. This hat of Daddy's is nowhere near that sentimental, and it wouldn't make him sad if I chewed it. But I know he would be a little upset with me. So, nope! I'm not going to take it. I am going to just leave it right where it's at. I know my daddy will be so happy that I made the right choice and left it alone because it's not mine. I just hope he never leaves his ice cream all alone within my reach. I am a doggie after all. I only have a certain amount of control. When it comes to ice cream

I have no control. I'm pretty sure I deserve a treat now. What say you, Mama?

Trust is built with consistency...

...and is the first step to loving another.

Mama Is Standing On The Bed!

Why is it that I am not allowed on the bed for any reason whatsoever? But Mama can stand on the bed! She says she is "dusting the headboard," and she couldn't reach it unless she stood on the bed. Well, I only lay on the bed, when I sneak in the bedroom, and she *has a cow*! That's a funny saying, isn't it? *Has a cow?* At least I don't think we have a cow!

But anyways, She is standing right on top of it! I think Mama makes up rules as she goes along to justify doing things she wants to do; that she won't let me do. Dusting the headboard! Please! She could have got on her knees. She didn't have to stand on the bed with her feet. She just knows how much fun it is but she won't let me do it. But I'm watching her every move and I'm telling Daddy when he gets home. My daddy never stands on the bed. He just sits on it or lays down and gets under the covers.

But NO! No one lets me on the bed. Now I'm mad at both of them. Am I, or am I not, a part of this family? I'm going to tell on both of them. Problem is, I don't have anyone else to tell. I guess I could tell my Littles. At least they let me lay on their beds. That's why they are my favorite. Mama, can the Littles come over?

Keeping Yona Alive

I was sitting here chewing on my new scarf minding my own business, like I always do. When I overheard Mama saying to Daddy, "It is taking all I can do to keep Yona alive the way she keeps eating everything in sight!" She said, "Yona!" That's me! What did she mean by that? I mean, maybe sometimes I eat things I am not supposed to eat…a lot. But to my defense, I am a doggie. That's what we do, we eat things. I'm sure I have said that before. Except, I won't eat scrambled eggs. They are gross. But I will eat mud pies and sticks. Go figure that. I guess we just like what we like. I also don't like bread, but I will eat paper towels. But I didn't eat glass I found that one time. I did try to eat a rock or two but Mama got on to me for that. They were not very good anyways so I let her have them. I do like to eat towels, anything with strings, and socks. Well, I guess Mama is right. She does have her hands full trying to keep me alive! I wonder when I am going to grow out of this "eating everything I get my mouth on stage?" Mama, maybe you should take this scarf off now. I sorta lost my appetite.

Deep Cleaning

Mama thought her house was hard to keep clean before the hurricane. Well, she is not a very *happy camper.* Why do humans use that phrase, anyways? I mean if camping is not fun why do it?

Mama acted like keeping the house clean was a huge chore before! She didn't have any idea just how bad it could really be until now. *Mud, mud, mud.* She keeps mumbling to herself as she sweeps and steams the tile that has been covered with mud. Not only my paw prints but everybody else's shoe prints that come in from the back area too. No one will take off their shoes before coming inside. Why are you looking at me? I'm just a doggie. I don't even wear shoes. Besides, I get hosed off every time by you and Daddy, if you manage to catch me before I run in that is. I don't see anyone else getting hosed off. Just saying…

Besides, I get the suspicious feeling Mama doesn't like mud as much as I do. I guess I may be the only one in the house that actually likes walking in it. I like the way it feels when it squishes between my toes, paw pads, or whatever they are called. I'm not even one year old yet. I don't really know the ins and outs of a doggie's anatomy.

But anyways back to Mama. Poor Mama, *hey, you missed a spot.* What!?! I'm just trying to help. She is so sensitive lately. Must be the mud.

Spending a few minutes cleaning is better than thinking about spending a whole day cleaning.

A Sad Day For Mama

Oct 8th, 2022, is a very sad day for Mama. Today is the one-year anniversary of her Mama's passing. My mama is sad a lot but I notice she is more quieter and teary-eyed today. She doesn't think I notice but I do. I can see and feel the hurt my mama has. It's just something we animals do. We can sense these things you know. I overheard her on the phone ordering a dozen yellow roses. I know yellow was Mawmaw Joyce's favorite color, so I'm sure she will really like them. She is also gathering up cleaning supplies to go clean around where Mawmaw Joyce and her husband, Pawpaw Bob, are.

I am going to try and stay really close to Mama today. I know it's going to be very hard on her. Especially because she is focusing all her thoughts and attention on today and the sad day, one year ago, when her mama went to Heaven. I know my mama will not be trying to redirect herself today so it's important I try to help her in any way I possibly can. I need to let my oldest big sister and my youngest big sister know just how Mama is feeling. But I have a feeling Mama wants to be left alone today. I guess she feels she needs to focus on her feelings and her mama and reflect on all the memories throughout all the years from days gone by. She is trying to hold on to all them memories. A tribute for Mawmaw Joyce today, if you will. I'm here for you Mama. Love you!

My Mawmaw Joyce bought this message plaque and left it for her husband Bob, my mama, and her three brothers Billy, Kenneth, and Rocky. She wrote on the package it was in. "To Bob and all my children, love Mama." She had no idea that Pawpaw Bob would pass before her, when she wrote his name on it. I thought it would be nice to share this with you all. Mawmaw Joyce wanted to let her husband and kids know there was a period of time to grieve and then they needed to go on with their lives and think happy thoughts instead of grieving and being sad all the time. Because she would be waiting for each of them when it was their time to go to heaven. That's going to be really hard for my mama. But I'm going to do my best to help Mama in any way I can today. She is my mama after all.

- To Those I Love -
When I am gone, just release me, let me go — so I can move into my afterglow. • You mustn't tie me down with your tears; let's be happy that we had so many years. • I gave you my love, you can only guess how much you gave me in happiness. I thank you for the love you each have shown, but now it's time I traveled on alone. So grieve for me awhile, if grieve you must, then let your grief be comforted with trust. • It's only for a while that we must part, so bless the memories within your heart. • And then, when you must come this way alone, I'll greet you with a smile and a "Welcome Home."

Who's There?

Hellooooo, peek-a-boo, I see you. You can't sneak up on me Daddy, I can hear really good, 'cause I'm a doggie and I can see all around me, and hear even better. So whatcha doing back there anyway? Do you need help? I'm a good helper. I can do a lot of things like carry sticks to the fire. But I can't go near the fire though because it's too dangerous with me being a doggie and all hairy and all. I could lick up any food that has been dropped on the ground. I enjoy that job a lot. It's a win-win really. I clean up the mess and get to eat good food too. Who wouldn't like that job?

So, what do you want to do, Daddy? We could go for a walk and see Sky down the road. I bet she has been missing me. My calendar is clear, just tell me what you want to do. You want to do a what!?! A boat ride! No way, no how, no sir! I am not getting on that floating death trap. I rather stay right here and lay on this cool tile floor because I know this is solid ground. That was a very disappointing answer, Daddy. I may need a treat for that while I lay here. The bacon ones will do just fine, thank you.

Boat ride... well, I never!

I'm Just Going To Say It

My playground stinks. Me being a doggie and saying that you know it's bad! I mean my playground is all gooey and muddy and fun and all. But, boy, oh boy, does it stink!!!!! It smells just like fishies! When I go out there, I have to get a bath every time! Mama and Daddy hose me down. I have never had so many showers in one day, in my whole life! I go out and get muddy, come in, and go into the shower room. Every time! And then I get hosed down. Oh, the shower room is really the breezeway blocked off with a gate. Then Mama and I fight over the towel for ten minutes or so because she tries to dry me off, and well, I want to play tug-of-war and eat the towel. But after all of that, I get to go inside, just to turn around and do it all over again.

So, I decided to play in Daddy's trailer this time so I can stay clean and not get all stinky and muddy and stuff. I found this little shove, maybe I can dig a trench to help get rid of some of the lake that is still in my playground. Because I can't take care of my business on Daddy's trailer! That wouldn't be nice. This is what you call being in a pickle. I don't get it. I couldn't even fit in a pickle, but that's how the saying goes, so they say. Boy, digging a trench is a hard and dirty job!

So, I guess it's going to be bath time again! Okay, Mama and Daddy here I come... get the hose and towel ready. Mean ol' Hurricane Ian. This is all your fault.

**Good ideas, like good pickles, are crisp,
enduring, and hard to make.
And oh by the way... pickles
are just cucumbers that believed in miracles.**

Mama Said I Stink!

My Mama says I STINK. I don't know about you but that kinda offended me. Why would someone just come out and say so boldly, "You stink!" And your mama of all people too! She must have heard me say my playground stinks and took a better sniff at me. But, I've never told her she stinks. Then again, I never saw her walking in the mud either.

To my defense, I wouldn't stink if my playground wasn't all muddy. I have to play on the high part of my playground to not get dirty. What Mama? What do you mean, "Not only do you stink, but you're dirty too?" I'm not dirty! No, I didn't go to the muddy area. What makes you think that? What do you mean I am getting too old to tell a fib?

Okay, I'm sorry Mama. You caught me with egg on my face. Why would anyone use that expression? I don't even like eggs. It's more like you caught me with mud on my face. I did sneak over to the muddy side, but to my defense, again, I thought I heard Griffin and wanted to say "hello." That's the truth, Mama.

I'm sorry I tried to pull the wool over your eyes, Mama. There we go again! Who does that? Pull the wool over your eyes! Will you forgive me, Mama? Okay, thank you! And, yes, I know. I'll go to the breezeway while you get the water hose. I know this routine really well now. I can't make any promises about the drying towel though. After all, I am a doggie. When will this nightmare be over? Okay, cleanish again, for now.

The truth prevails,
it always finds its way out.

But, The Birds Though!

It really wasn't my fault! Mama had to work and she let me outside just for a minute to take care of my business before she got on the phone to work. And there were birds everywhere in my playground. You know them big white ones with the yellowish/orange-looking beaks. I can't tell color well 'cause I'm a doggie. But anyways, I took off running like a hunting dog after the birds. Mama is just a yelling, "Yona No!!" That's me, Yona. Mama just doesn't understand the joy in chasing birds. I just couldn't help myself; the mud was flying in every direction.

Well, Mama had to get on the phone, so guess what! Yep! I'm stuck outside 'till my Daddy can come wash me off. But he will have to catch me or outsmart me first because I don't like baths. Well, Daddy was outside working in the yard so he figured seeings I would not come in, that he would just leave me outside as long as he stayed out. Boy, oh boy mud here I come. I played and played and played. Shhh, don't tell Mama though. She is already a little upset that I didn't listen to her command and stop when she told me to stop.

Well, I washed off most of the mud running in the water and I'm now hiding behind the tree on the high side of my playground cause, Daddy and Mama are at the door staring me down. I guess this is it. Wish me luck!

But Mama, the Birds though!

It's important to listen…
…that is why God gave us two ears
and only one mouth!

Where Did My Playground Go?

Mama, I just have one question. Where did my playground go? I guess there are always consequences for your actions. Seeings Mama nor Daddy can take me out without me running through the mud. They are blocking off every part of my playground that has mud in it and now I only have a small area I can go to. This is terrible!

Mama takes me for walks when she can and that is nice and all. But I have to be on a leash because, well, I clearly do not listen at times and Mama doesn't want to take any chances of me running down to the road and getting hurt.

But anyways back to my playground, if only I had listened to Mama like I was supposed to in the first place. I would have a lot more freedom now. But, live and learn. My mama said I cannot keep getting into all that mud. She and Daddy cannot stay outside trying to chase me down in what's left of the lake in my playground.

So this was their only choice, she said. I guess it will mean less baths for me and Mama said a lot less mess for her to clean up. Plus I have destroyed two towels already. I said it before and I'll say it again...these teenage years are rough! Mamas and Daddys, take it easy on the teens. I'm talking from experience when I say, "They know not what they do!" It's like something has taken over our teenage minds and bodies. So, think before you act.

They will grow out of it, just like me. I hope so anyway. In the meantime, just look at how messy our place still is. My poor Daddy has his work cut out for him. He is still working on the front. We had a huge mess everywhere. I don't think I like these hurricanes.

Let Me Dry My Face Off First

I didn't get muddy this time Mama. Just my face got a little wet because of the rain and me trying to catch that bug. I couldn't help it. I had to go outside. I'll be in, in just a minute. Just let me dry my face off first. What do you mean, I need to dry off everything, even my paws. Well, you are going to have to help me do that. I can dry my front paws off but the towel is too high to dry off my back paws. I'm not a contortionist you know. Besides, you get mad when I bite at the towel when you try to dry me off. But we can give it a whirl if you want. I'll do my best not to bite the towel but I am not promising anything.

We could just dry my legs off if you want. What do you mean, I can't come in the house if I don't dry off completely? Have you seen my coat? It's thick! This will take forever!

Okay, okay, go ahead and dry me off because I'm getting hungry. I thought drying my face off by myself would get your attention. I thought you would be happy and proud of me for doing that! But I can see now, it will take a lot more than drying my own face to impress you. Mama, you really should give me praise when I do good things, and then maybe I will start doing good things more often.

If I am constantly getting in trouble, for things I do wrong and not getting praised for doing some things right, then how am I ever going to learn? Plus it makes me sad. Boy, you sure are a tough cookie sometimes, Mama. Speaking of cookies. Do we have any?

In the grand scheme of cookies...

...Mommas and Daddies are the chocolate chips!

Which Way Did They Go?

My Littles are getting so big! I love them so much, and I wish they lived here all the time with me. We would play all day long from sun up to sun down and then some. But today they are here! First, we are going to play, "Pet Yona." Then we are going to play, "Yona Obeys a Command and Gets a Treat." Then we are going to play, "Yona Fetch." We are going to play all them games today as soon as they eat breakfast, brush their teeth and hair, and get dressed.

It's going to be all about me today! Hey, did anyone see which way my Littles went? One minute we were sitting on the steps, and the next minute they were in the kitchen getting breakfast. Then poof they were gone. I just turned my head for one second to get a treat from Mama. Then, the next thing I knew. They were gone. Hey Littles, come out and play! I will not make it all about me. I will play what you want to play too. I'm sorry I was being so selfish. I promise I will not do it again. We will all take turns picking a game, okay? Oh, goodie goodie goodie, here they come! I hope you all have a nice day and play fair. Let everyone have a chance to do what they want to do. Enjoy your day. I know I will.

But Daddy Left The Doors Open

I don't know why everyone is so upset with me. I wasn't the one who left the side door open and the garage door up! I mean, it's not my fault I wanted to go exploring, and my playground is all muddy...still! Besides, SOMEONE, and I will not mention any names (DADDY), cut out my only means of outdoor entertainment when he blocked off my playground. Well, I guess I did name names. Oh well.

And, oh, by the way, it is most certainly not my fault you didn't bring a rotisserie chicken to try and get me back home, Mama. Well, maybe I did run from you both each time you got within arms reach, and maybe there was a tiny instance there when Mama almost fell trying to catch me. But to my defense. I thought you two were playing tag. How was I to know?

These rules to this whole getting out thing is all kinda iffy to me. I ran fast, didn't I, Daddy? Why are you looking at me like that? You're as bad as Mama. It was nice to see Sky again, wasn't it? And Ms. Barbara's house even though no one was home. Sorry, Ms. Barbara, be careful where you step 'cause I may or may not have left something behind while I was in a fast trot playing "catch me if you can" with Mama and Daddy. It's all kind of a blur because I was running so fast at times.

Mama didn't have time to grab a bag. She didn't even bring an appropriate treat for the game. Mama will go down later and assess the situation. Brady wasn't home, either. As a matter of fact, I didn't see any of my friends except Sky. But I was in a big hurry and could only say a quick hello because Mama and Daddy were hot on my trail. Well, they cornered me and brought me back home. Boy, was that exhausting! I'm going to rest now. I bet Daddy never leaves the doors open again. Just saying…

But I Just Wanted Ice Cream

I Just wanted Ice Cream. How else was I supposed to let her know I wanted my doggie ice cream? I only nipped her toe to get her attention so I could walk to the freezer, and she would know exactly what I wanted. I know where she keeps it.

How was I supposed to know she would scream that loud? It was barely a flesh wound. Mama is a crybaby. And do you know I never got my ice cream? She scolded me right then and there, saying it was unacceptable behavior on my part. What!?! It was just a love nibble. All I wanted was ice cream! I had been standing here waiting FOREVER!!!! But did you acknowledge me? NO!?!?! So what else was I to do? I am just a doggie you know. And! You get on to me every time I bark continuously for attention.

Oh, I forgot to tell you all. I bark now. But only when I want some attention. A doggies gotta do what a doggies gotta do. But anyways, where was I? Oh yeah, I'm sorry, Mama, if I bit you too hard. But to my defense, if you had not jerked your foot away, it wouldn't have hurt nearly as bad. You will learn in time, Mama. So how bout that ice cream now, hmmm? Okay! Okay! I'm going. Boy, you sure are touchy here lately. It must be your diet. What? I'm going, I'm going. So, no ice cream?

What About My Tongue?

Well, I may have dug just a little bit, but I didn't get dirty, though. What about my tongue? I don't see any dirt on my tongue. I don't feel or taste any dirt on my tongue. Mama, I think you are exaggerating. What do you mean you can't see my tongue? It's right here, attached to my face! Everybody's tongue is attached to their face. I'm a doggie, and I even know that. Oh, you can't see my tongue for all the dirt!

Why don't you ever try to find the good in things, Mama? You are such a pessimist. I, on the other hand, am very optimistic. I see the good in almost every situation except my playground. Don't get me started with that. But anyway, you need to be more positive in your thinking. I mean, so my tongue may have just a tad bit of dirt on it, so you say. But the good news is, I am not dirty anywhere else. You want to check my paws or my tail, or my belly. See, all clean. Maybe a smidge on the side of my face, but I don't see where that warrants a bath.

Come on, Mama, step out of the box a little. Live on the edge. Be a rebel. Let's skip the bath this time.

I'll go drink some water and wash this so-called mud off my tongue. You know, Mama, a stress-free life is way more healthier for you. You should try it sometime. Why just look at me? I'm just as carefree as they come. Well, until you mention a bath, anyway. And, well, there is my muddy playground also.

Oh no, now look at what you have done. I may need a treat to make me feel better 'cause you're starting to rub off on me. The bacon one, please. Thank you. I feel better now. You should eat one of my bacon treats; maybe you will feel better too. Just saying…

It's My 11th Month Birthday

Can you believe this? Eleven months old today! I'm so close to being a year old I can taste it. I wonder if I will feel any differently. Being one whole year old and all. I'm so excited about that. But I guess I should concentrate on my eleventh-month birthday first. Just look at the toys I got! Boy, oh boy, I love toys. I'm so happy. I think I might cry tears of joy.

Mama and Daddy buy the best toys! I cannot decide which one I like best. I keep trying them all one at a time. I have ran in circles, jumped around, flipped over backwards even, playing with all these toys. I overheard Daddy ask Mama if she got me some ice cream for my birthday, and she said, "YES!!!! "Oh boy, oh boy, best eleventh-month birthday ever!

I heard my Littles were coming over later today to play with me for my birthday. I can't wait to see them. I wonder if they are going to bring me a present? It's okay if they don't. I just love to see them because they are my best friends and I love them. One more month to go. Can you believe that! Happy Birthday To Me! So, about that ice cream, Mama.

Whatcha Got To Eat Kayla?

Hurry Kayla, give me some food before Mama comes. Whatcha got to eat up here anyways? Hey, there's nothing up here! What's in that cup? Oh no, here she comes. Stay calm and quiet and play like you are petting me. Maybe she will not notice I'm begging for food. 'Cause I'm not supposed to be up here, because I was taught patience and sit.

But seeings you haven't really given me any of these commands. I didn't do them. So technically, if I get in trouble, it will most likely be all your fault because, well, you're older than me, and you knew the right commands to keep me from getting on the counter. But you didn't use them. So, I will have to tell on you. That's only if I get caught, though, okay? Just keep petting me and hope she doesn't notice.

Mama, I can explain. I was sitting there minding my own business, and Kayla called me up here to pet me. Right, Kayla? Kayla, right? Oh no, Kayla, you told on me.

What do you mean it's not nice to tell a fib? Okay, okay, Kayla. You are right. Mama, I'm sorry I was trying to get Kayla to fib for me. And Kayla, I'm sorry that I put you in that bad, uncomfortable situation with Mama.

If you start fibbing and people get to where they don't trust you. Then you will be like the boy who called, "wolf." (Y'all, I just can't make this stuff up!) Kayla, you were smart, to tell the truth. Now Mama will trust you, and I know that it's a good feeling to have people trust you. I'm sorry, Kayla. I will not ever do that to you again. I hope you can forgive me. Love you, Kayla. Sorry, Mama. I will try not to be like the boy who cried wolf. Even though I don't even know what "cried wolf" means. Maybe it's a human thing. So, can I have a treat?

Brady Time

Mama and I went for a much-needed walk, and look who we ran into...Brady! It seems like forever since I saw you last. You live right next door, and because our fence is not right next to each other, because my daddy built my playground on the other side of our yard. I don't get to see you as much as I would like.

Only when Mama and I go for a walk, and that's if you are outside at the time. We need to plan some play dates, Brady. Ask your mama and daddy if you can come over to my playground and play with me. When it dries up, that is. Mean ole Hurricane Ian made a mess of everything. But anyways. Then I can take this leash off, and we can run really fast. I can't run fast with this leash on because the other end is attached to my mama, and she is so slow when it comes to running down the road.

She can run really fast if she sees I'm in danger, like with the lawn mower incident. I'll tell you all about it when my playground is fixed and you come over to play. I will also see if Mama will give us some doggie ice cream if your mama says it's okay. I'm so excited. I can't wait! I hope you can come over soon. I miss you. I better go now. We have to get all our exercising in because I have an appointment with the groomers today. Tomorrow is my mama and my second book signing. That's going to be fun. I get to meet a lot of nice people, and Miss Tammy is spending the night with us tonight. I just love her. She is so sweet.

Okay, bye for now, Brady. Okay, Mama, I'm ready. Let's do this.

In times of joy,
we all wish we had a tail to wag!

Watcha Doing Over There?

Why do you have my toys? You know, I am down to about four or five, including the ones I got for my 11th-month birthday. Because you and Mama have not so nicely thrown all of my other toys away. What are you doing with the few I have left? There is nothing wrong with them. I check them every night. Not one of them are damaged. Well, not much. So, why are you messing with them? I see…they were in your way. Okay, that's a good answer. So, what are you going to do with them? Oh yes, that's a good spot right there. Thank you, Daddy, for putting them in a safe spot. For a minute there, I was worried they were going to the place of no return. You know, The trash! It's a good thing you two bought me some new toys for my birthday, or I wouldn't have hardly any toys at all.

Do you think you can get Mama to go on her phone and order me some more? That shouldn't be hard, seeings she is ALWAYS on that phone of hers. I know why she is always on her phone. I just wish humans would think about their kids and furbabies a little more and maybe put their phones down for a while. I mean, we will only be young for so long. Something for all you parents to chew on there. Do you like how I phrased that? Just saying…but anyways, thank you, Daddy, for saving my toys and putting them in a safe spot. Now, step away from them, now…if you don't mind. Just in case you get any ideas. Thank you, Daddy. Love you.

Book Signing #2

What a great day we had yesterday. Me, my Mama, and Tammy. We went to our second book signing. I met some of the nicest people, and we all had our pictures taken together. It is so nice to have so many friends come and visit me. Like I said before, it makes you feel all warm and fuzzy inside to know so many people like you. It's a really good feeling.

When you are nice to people and treat people with respect. Then people are nice back to you. If I was to treat people mean and not respect them, then they would not like me and not respect me back. So always remember to treat people like you want to be treated. That includes talking bad about others and making others feel bad in front of a lot of other people. You wouldn't want that to happen to you, would you?

So, surround yourself with nice people because nobody likes a bully. Just remember, besides your family, your friends will be the next important people in your life. So always be kind.

Because being nice takes way less effort than being well, not so nice.

So, back to my book signing. I am so glad I got to meet some of the nicest people. I even got to meet the cutest little "Little" named Tatum. Aka, "Sweet T." Thank you to the Split Ends Salon for allowing us to have our book signing there. I am so humbled by all of the love and support everyone gives my Mama and me. What a great day it was.

Goodbye Kisses

Tammy had to leave to go home, because, even though she loves to visit, everyone knows there's just no place like home. We had the best time while she was here. I played with her a lot! Then I rested, and Mama, Daddy, and Tammy talked and reminisced about days gone by. Then we played some more, and we had ice cream, and then I got petted for hours and hours. Boy, oh boy, I really enjoy it when we have company.

It's like having a live toy to enjoy for a day or so. If I had my way, we would have company every night. But, Mama and Daddy said everyone is busy and can't always stay the night with us. They said people have to work to pay for a place to live and buy food and clothes and things like that. I had no idea!

Then they said all the littles had to go to school to learn so they could get good jobs. I didn't realize every human, child, and adult had a goal to obtain in life. Oh, man being a human must be hard work. I am going to start being a lot nicer to humans, big and small. They are very busy people. It puts a new perspective on the way I look at them. No wonder people nowadays say they are just too busy.

But also, they need to remember to always take time to call or visit the ones they love because one day they might look around and their loved one will not be there. So, never be too busy to at least tell your loved ones how much you love them. It doesn't matter how young you are. Call your loved ones. They will be so happy, and one day you will be glad you did. So, I love you, Tammy. I can't wait to see you next month. Bye for now, here are some goodbye kisses. See you soon!

Poor Mama Is Losing It!

So here I am underneath the dining room table where I pretty much am every day when Mama has to work. I was just chilling, minding my own business just like I always do. When all of a sudden, I hear Mama yell, "Oh No!" The chair scoots back really fast, and my Mama goes running to the back door, yelling, "Yona! Yona! Where are you, baby!" My mama called me "baby." That's funny, but I'm not a baby. I'm not even a puppy anymore. I'm a big doggie.

But anyways, then, she frantically started searching the inside of the house for me. I just layed right here because I knew eventually she would look under here and find me. Finally, she squatted down and said with a somewhat happy, shaking voice, "Yona! There you are!" Mama was so happy she found me safe under the dining room table because she let me outside a long time ago, and I guess she forgot she let me back in.

Poor Mama is losing it. She must be working way too hard. Either that, or I am just a very quiet, good doggie, and Mama forgets I'm here. I don't know, but either way, I'll just ride it out and let her do her thing. I figure there is no sense in getting excited over it. She does this a lot, so you get used to it after a while. Hey, Mama, yes, it's me, right here where I have been for the past hour since you let me in. Poor Mama. I sure do love her.

Thank You Ms. Stacee

During my second book signing, Ms. Stacee, one of my most bestest friends, gave my mama a gift to buy me a present. Thank You, Ms. Stacee! Look at what I got with it? Boy, oh boy, are these fun to play with! They are kinda like my mama's weights but lighter and way cooler than her weights. These toys produce treats! Mama's weights don't do that. I have chewed and chewed and chewed on these all day and really enjoyed them. You just can't go wrong with the friends I have.

Ya know, it's not just about the toys, although they are very nice. I appreciate all the friends I have made. This journey I have taken with my mama and daddy and my family at my side has been some of the best times I believe any doggie could ever have. Just think! I have met more people and more four-legged friends than I could have ever imagined. I have had adventure after adventure, some good, some bad. But what a life I have had so far. I can't wait to see what is in store for me this next month. It is anybody's guess, really. I know whatever life brings my way. I will have my family and friends at my side to share it with them. And oh, what a wonderful life it is! Thank you again, Ms. Stace…I love you!

It Was Fun 'Til It Wasn't

Well, it all started when Daddy came home from the grocery store. Mama was on the phone working and Daddy had his hands full, so he couldn't shut the door. I was inching my way to the back door when Daddy said, "Yona," that's me, Yona. "Don't go out there! Because I didn't close the doors to the garage."

I mean! REALLY!!!! What did he expect me to do? The chase was on! Could it be true? Yes, it is! The breezeway door was open, and the garage door was up! Look out, world, here I come again. Well, it was fun 'til it wasn't, but I didn't know it at the time.

Even the neighbors were trying to help catch me. Ms. Barbara was calling me, trying to get me, and even her little doggie Bridget was helping. Bridget was informing me I was not behaving in an appropriate manner, in her doggie way of speaking. Mr. Bill was telling them where I was, and even their house painter tried to catch me. Ms. Nancy was riding Sky, her horse, and they even joined in. That part was fun.

What I didn't know was Mama had got in her car and was going to drive down and try to get me to jump in the back seat; because I like doing that. Well, Mama was in such a frazzled state she either didn't wait for the garage door to go all the way up, or it got stuck, one or the other. But anyways, Mama ran right into the garage door with the back of her car! I was just thinking, "it was all fun and games," 'til they caught me and brought me home. And then I saw the garage door. Oh, and Daddy got a nasty tear on his hand too. I think that was me that done that because I was so excited.

But anyways, the garage door is messed up pretty bad. I think Mama's car faired okay. They will have to have it checked out. Even though this really wasn't ALL my fault. There is always consequences to your actions. I could have stopped when my daddy said to stop. But I didn't. Now Mama's car and the garage door is wrecked, and it would have never happened if I had done as I was told. And daddy wouldn't have a cut on his hand right now.

It is important to always stop and think before you act. Think about how things will affect others. If only I had done that. Things would have turned out differently. I'm sorry, Mama, sorry, Daddy. I didn't mean to cause all this trouble. Can you ever forgive me? P.S. The trainer is scheduled to come in a few days to help us with our issues. I hope she can help.

Why Are You Looking At Me Like That?

Hey Daddy, why are you looking at me like that? I said I was sorry. I didn't mean to hurt your hand. I guess my paw scratched up against your skin when we were playing "catch me if you can." At least, that's what I thought we were playing. Daddy, I would never hurt you on purpose. I feel so bad about your hand. If I could take it back, I would. I have been a good girl since it all happened. I didn't bark as much as I usually do while you and Mama were watching TV last night. I did try to get your pizza, well, only once. But to my defense, I am a doggie, you know. I did eat all my food and cleaned up all my toys. Okay, maybe I didn't clean up all my toys, but I thought about it! If someone hadn't thrown my toy basket away, I might have picked them up. Okay, you're right. I wouldn't have. I will share my toys with you if you want. Help me out here, Daddy. I'm grasping at straws here. What a strange saying, "grasping at straws," where did that come from? I guess what I am trying to say is, "I love you so much, Daddy, and I didn't mean to hurt your hand. It was an accident. Please forgive me. You are one of my bestest friends in the whole wide world. You do a lot for me, and I just want to say thank you, Daddy." What do you say? Will you forgive me? You will! Thank you so much, Daddy. So, do you want to play? I'll even let you pick the game. Oh boy, oh boy, oh boy! Let's play!

Forgiveness is a gift!

There is no love without forgiveness,

and there is no forgiveness without love!

The Trial Run

Mama and Daddy felt so bad for me after the disastrous occurrence that happened the other day. You know, my joy run. But anyways, Mama and Daddy felt bad because they know I really don't have much room to play. So... guess what they did? They opened up my playground so I could run freely for a little while. They said it was a trial run 'cause even though it has dried up a lot. There is still a good portion of mud scattered about. They were hoping that I would only play on one side and stay out of the mud.

So, okay, let me get this straight... just stay to the left of the playground, and everything will be okay? Did I just hear what I thought I heard? Well, okay, let's see. Here I go! Good job so far... to the left, the left, Yona, you can do this. Oh, man, which way is left again?

Oh well, HELLO, PLAYGROUND, MY OLD FRIEND! I ran and ran and ran. But I never laid down or wallered in the mud. No sir, I stayed on my feet the whole time. Well, Mama was working, and Daddy was supposed to be watching me. Well, he was watching me, all right. He watched me run through all that mud, and you would not believe what he did next! HE LET ME IN THE HOUSE! And then he went and told Mama my feet were all muddy! Hey Daddy, you got that a little backwards, didn't you? Mama took one look at my muddy feet, and out the door, I went. To the bathhouse, I go! It's better known as the water hose.

Why am I happy, you ask? Well, I'll tell you. I am so close to getting my playground back that I can taste it. Maybe not really taste it. Well, maybe just a little. Happy days are ahead; I just know it. I love you, playground!

The Toilet Paper

I don't understand, Mama and Daddy always shut the bathroom door. I figured they left it open for me so I could find new toys to play with. Well, my eyes got as big as half-dollars when I walked around the corner and saw this white, soft roll of fluff on the wall, AND IT SPINS TOO!!!

How exciting is this! I had the best time ever! Did you know that after the white fluffy stuff is all gone, there's this chewable tube thingy you can chew on? It's a two-for-one toy! Well, that was fun. Now I need to go rest for a while.

Uh oh, I hear Daddy and Mama talking very loudly. Daddy is talking about something called toilet paper. He said it was all over the floor. Hey Daddy, the only thing that was on the floor was some white fluffy stuff and that roller thingy. Well, I'm pretty sure that roller thingy will never be found. At least not for a few days, anyway. And not in the same shape, it was in either.

Do you have any more of them fluffy toys you are calling toilet paper? Where can I get some more of this toilet paper you're speaking of? What do you mean it's not a toy? You do *what* with it? Ew! I had that in my mouth! I eat a lot of things, but I don't eat things associated with that end of the anatomy. Well, not on purpose, anyway.

Mama, I may need some water to wash this down with. Maybe a treat will help me feel better too. The good bacon ones, please. Who leaves things like that out within reach of a doggie? How gross! Mama, will you wipe my mouth out? Please!

Mama, We're Waiting

Kayle and I smell sausage! I was first in line, and Kayle was second. We get first dibs. I'm not too fond of this big bowl of slimy-looking balls of sunshine in this glass bowl, though. Kayle, what is that? Eggs! Oh no, no, no! Mama gave me some one time, and they were gross. I don't like eggs or bread. I'll just have the sausage, please. What do you mean I eat dirt and bugs? What does that have to do with anything, Kayle?

You like what you like, and you don't like what you don't like. Simple as that. Anyways, I don't actually eat the bugs. I just catch them with my mouth, and as you are well aware! I don't have hands to hold them with, and my paws will only corner them. It's my mouth that carries them. But anyways, let's get back to this sausage. When are they going to be done, Mama?

Kayle won't let me jump up on the stove to see for myself. She said something about safety first. I guess she's right 'cause I don't want to burn my paws on the hot stove. Kayle, count how many is in there so we know how many we can have. Hey Mama, whatcha doing? Whatcha got there? Dog food! Really! But what about the sausage, though? What about the emergency room visit? Are you really going to bring that up now? Oh, all right. I don't want to go through all that again. But there better be some bacon treats in that dog food. Kayle, it looks like you moved up to first in line. Okay, Mama, show me the bacon.

Drop It!

So. You all know I like to play tug-of-war, and on occasion, I like to play fetch in the house. My issue is, when I have my ball or bone, I will not let go of it to play fetch because, well, I want to play tug-of-war with it. My Mama had this great idea that she was going to teach me to drop my balls and bones because, well, that's where most of the injuries occur. When Mama and Daddy or whoever is playing with me, they try to get my ball or bone, I hurry and try to get a better grip on it and oops…there is where it happens. It is inevitable that someone is going to yell and loudly! What!?!?! Don't yell at me, I can't help it. I thought we were playing tug-of-war.

Well, anyways, Mama decided she was going to teach me "drop it." She went and got a bacon treat. A Bacon Treat! I don't know why she thought this was going to be a good idea, but here we go. "Yona, drop it," says Mama. Umm. I don't even have it. I want that treat. She starts trying to stick my bone in my mouth. But I'm like. "Nope! I want the bacon treat." I'm holding firmly onto the bone, which should have been a very noticeable clue that I clearly wanted my bone and the treat.

After several failed attempts, I decided, okay, if it will get me that bacon treat, I'll try it. So I put the bone in my mouth, and when I saw the bacon treat, I spit out my bone before Mama could say, "drop it." I told you this wasn't going to go well. Even Daddy was shaking his head.

After about ten minutes of Mama trying to stick the bone in my mouth and me trying to hold the bone down, Mama gave up and just fed me the whole bacon treat. I told you it wouldn't end well for you, Mama. Better luck next time. Now, do you want to play tug-of-war, I mean fetch?

Nobody Came

I barked and barked. I jumped up and hit the door. I scratched and scratched and barked some more, and still, nobody came. What is happening around here? I know I can't be the center of attention 24/7 but come on! Please don't leave me outside begging like an animal! Um, scratch that last part.

Anyways, let me in, please! If you want me to beg, I will beg. Mama, this is me begging! Let me in! Oh, Thank you for opening the door. Whew, I thought I was going to have to stay out here all night! How did I get out here, you say? Daddy came out to feed the fish and left the door cracked, and I snuck out. Poor daddy had no idea. He just came back in and shut the door on me. So, I did what doggies do and plundered around for a minute or two.

Mama, I appreciate you opening the door and letting me in and all. But didn't you forget something in the process? You know the game. I sit here and wait for a treat, and I don't come in until I get one. And I most certainly don't see a treat in your hand! Hey, why did you shut the door back? Mama! Hey Mama! Where did you go? I'm sorry, I will come in without a treat. Please let me in. I promise if you open the door I'll come in like a good girl.

Oh, thank you, thank you, thank you, Mama. I tell ya, you sure are a tough cookie sometimes. Hey, a cookie sounds good. Can I have one of them? What? I came in, didn't I? Boy, the older you get, I mean, you sure do look nice tonight, Mama!

**You'll get more bees with honey
than with vinegar!**

Hello Miss Laura, Trainer Lady

Hello Miss Laura, I'm so glad you're here. We are desperate! Are you here to train Mama and Daddy? They need a lot of help trying to take care of me in the manner that a Siberian Husky is accustomed to. Whoa, who's that leash for? Hey! Did you bring one for Mama and Daddy too? They are the ones who forgot all you taught them. How do they expect me to behave right if they don't know the proper commands?

I mean, a carpenter can't build a house without tools. (I made that up all by myself!) What are you looking at, Mama? I don't know how I became the one with the issues. See! Yes, trainer lady, you tell them. Are you listening, Mama and Daddy? Laura, the trainer lady, said you two have let me run this house. You have let me take over. Now, whose fault is that?

Hmmm. I wonder? I mean, I'm just a doggie, so you two tell me. Who's the problem child around here? Me or you two? Preach, trainer lady preach! She said it was all three of us for those of you in the back row.

Hey, wait a minute. All three of us? Well, then, they should have to wear a leash too. Whatever happened to equal opportunity? And so it began... We worked on putting the leash on and taking the leash off. Putting the leash on and taking the leash off. Over and over and over. And I couldn't throw myself to the ground, bite the leash or jump up on Mama or we would have to start all over again.

I was so tired of having to behave that I slept for the rest of the day afterwards! And the worst part was, WE NEVER WENT FOR A WALK!!!!! Laura, the trainer lady, said my mama and Daddy need to treat me just like they would treat their kids. What? So whatever their kids didn't get away with, then I can't either? But did that mean I could sleep on the beds and eat at the table? That would be a big No! I think this was a one-sided training day today. But next time Laura, the trainer lady, comes, I think mama should wear the leash. Just saying.

P.S. Mama took me out later that evening before dark, and we played fetch on the high side of my playground. That was fun! I ran and ran and ran. Thank you, Mama.

Just Try It, Mama

Come on, it will be fun. Just close one eye at a time. It don't matter which one. So can you see your nose now? Look toward your nose. See it? How cool is that? Now, where is your peripheral vision? It's gone, right? Now try it with the other eye. Yes, that eye. Keep it closed. Longer, longer, just a little longer. Hey, you peaked! What do you mean, what do I have? I don't have anything. Oh, you mean this little paper towel? It was just lying here, and I was keeping an eye on it for you. So, why is it in my mouth? Well, because I don't have hands like you and Daddy, so I was holding it in my mouth for you.

You don't buy it, do you? Humans and their phrases. Gotta love it. But anyways, the truth is...I wanted it so badly, and you dropped it by your side next to me, and I figured if I grabbed it, you would surely see it with your peripheral vision. So, I decided to try and trick you by playing a game. If I could get you to close your left eye. You wouldn't see me get the paper towel. I'm sorry, Mama. It was a dirty trick. Although I didn't see any dirt.

But anyways, here it is. You can have it. I'm sorry I was trying to trick you. I'm kinda full anyways because I played with Daddy earlier and I ate his paper towel. Poor Daddy, he just won't ever learn, will he, Mama? So, tell the truth. How many of you tried it?

What Little Ball?

Do you mean the little ball that was in this blue toy that I have in my mouth? The little ball that was impossible to get out of here? The one you bought me and was supposed to be supervising me while I played with it to make sure I didn't get the little ball out?

Daddy, do you and Mama EVER communicate? That little Ball was out the first week you bought it for me. I worked and worked and worked on this until I finally got it out. Mama was listening and watching me with that peripheral vision of hers. Do you know she waited until little pieces started to come out before she grabbed it from me? She let me work on it for hours while she worked, and for what? Just so she could get the prize.

I laid quiet as a mouse chipping away on it. Now that's one animal I haven't met yet. But anyways, I was so quiet and chewed on it faithfully until I started getting my teeth in between the wheels just right to fray the ball just enough to get the fabric and pull. I pulled until I got to the rubbery part, then I worked frantically until I got the ball cracked open. Then I started pulling and pulling until the ball ripped into small enough pieces to come out.

But then Mama came over and took my ball! I think that was mean, don't you, Daddy? What do you mean she did that on purpose? She did it to keep me occupied? Well, it sure did that. But why take the prize I worked so hard for? I wasn't going to swallow the rubber ball. Oh, who am I kidding? I was going to eat it like it was a chocolate-covered cherry. Although I have never had a chocolate-covered cherry. Do you think you could get me one, Daddy? I sure would like to try one. What do you mean? Chocolate is bad for doggies.

Oh well, will you buy me another one of these tire toys with the ball inside then? I won't try to get the ball out next time. I know...even I thought that was funny. We both know that isn't true. Okay then, how about a treat? The bacon one, please. Thank you, Daddy. If you buy me another one of these, it can be just our little secret, okay? Now, where's that bacon?

Too Cold To Swim

Kayle, Kayla, you have got to be kidding me! I am a Siberian Husky, and I wouldn't even get in that cold water. Well, to tell the truth, I wouldn't get in it if it was like bath water. But that's besides the point. Aren't you two cold? Is that why you are on that raft? If you are on the raft to stay out of the cold water, then why get in the pool, to begin with?

I will never understand why you two do the things you do. Any human, as far as that goes. Mama talks to herself because I have heard her. Daddy wears a funny black thing in his ears that dangles like a necklace, and he won't let me play with it. He said it's to hear the TV better, so who knows?

But anyways, about this cold water. You know Summer is over, right? It's November now. Who said you can swim all year round in Florida? What do you mean that's the rules? There are way too many rules to follow, and try to keep them all straight. I'm just going to watch you two struggle on that float as you try to not touch that water. This is not a game I want to play, but it seems you two are having fun. So, to each their own, I guess. Enjoy your game, even if it is a silly one. I mean, have fun, you two. Maybe when you get done with that game, we can play chase, okay? I like that game a lot. So I'll just wait here patiently until you are done. Just to refresh my memory, how long is "patiently" again?

Difficulties disappear and obstacles vanish

with the magical effect of

patience and perseverance.

The Kitchen Counter Treasures

Wow, the treasures I have discovered on the kitchen counters are even beyond my expectation. So far, I have taken two hand towels: One has a new home out in Daddy's rag box, and the other one my Mama saved. Then I got two paper towels and one red dishcloth. So, now my mama is having a cleaning-off and decluttering frenzy. Running around like a chicken with her head cut off. Can we just stop and picture that last sentence for a moment? On second thought, maybe it's best we didn't.

But anyways, my Daddy was filling the paper towel dispenser, so he pulled it to the edge of the counter, and then HE LEFT THE ROOM! He just makes this stuff too easy for me. Mama was on the phone like she ALWAYS is, and saw me frantically trying to grab something, anything at this point. Because I couldn't pull down the dispenser like I had hoped. But the red dishcloth caught my eye. I guess that was the straw that broke the camel's back. Now, let me just take a minute to reflect on that last statement. Can you visualize that? But anyways...Mama got off the phone and got her red dishcloth back!

When I tell you she was moving and organizing and talking to herself all at the same time, I got tired just watching her, so I just went and laid down. I was afraid to get in her way. She would glare over at me a few times with her forehead all wrinkled up and her eyes all big and bugging out looking, and her lips all tight and all. I don't think I have ever seen that look before. I gotta say, Mama, that's not a very flattering look on you at all. What? I'm just making an observation over here. I need to ask my sisters Kari and Kara about this look. I mean, should I be concerned?

After my Mama got done, there was nothing on the counters. I mean, not even the treats she gives me. Everything was put away. She even put up the Fall decorations. What wasn't put away was all the way up against the wall. It wasn't anything I wanted anyways. Coffee pot, toaster, air fryer, things like that. But no hand towels, dish towels, paper towels, and no treats. Mama is a bit of an extremist if you ask me. Although no one asked me. Why, she even took the runners off the table and server in the dining room. I never once touched them. But they would have made good tug-of-war runners, though. Oh well, I guess the trainer will be coming back soon. Hey Mama, at least your kitchen's all clean now. What? She can be so touchy at times.

Excuse Me But...

Hello Mama, Mama, Mama, yoohoo! Hey, down here. See me, Mama? I'm trying to get your attention. Look down. There you go. Peek-a-boo, I see you. Ummm, excuse me, but this was the only way I could get your attention. Do you know what time it is? It's time to quit working and play with me. You said soon. Is it soon yet? You know I need all the playful stimulation I can get. Just ask the vet and trainer lady. They will tell you. So come on, daylight's wasting. I got my ball and tug-of-war rope ready!

After that, maybe we can go for a walk? You know I need all the practice I can get walking with my leash on. So what do you say, Mama? Let's go! What do you mean you still have over three hours left to work? It feels like you have been working forever. Remember, I'm on doggie time here. Call your boss and tell her you need to take a play day off. Because I need you to play with me. Do you realize I am almost one whole year old!

In eleven more days, it will be my birthday. Oh boy, oh boy, I will get to have a big birthday party. Woohoo! But anyways, you are missing out on all my childhood, or should I say doggiehood years. Is doggiehood even a word?

But anyways, I am just going to rest my head right here 'til you are done, if that's okay. As long as it's soon. I hope soon is not as long as patiently. Is it Mama?

Never mind a little dirt...
...having fun is much more important.

Me And My Playground

Mama and Daddy understand why I have been doing a lot of things which are a little out of character even for me. It's because I haven't been able to release much of this "Husky Energy" I have. They had to block my playground off for a while. Well, you know my daddy took down the barrier and let me go play in it as a trial run the other day. Let's just say I had fun with a capital "F"! They have been letting me back out in it little by little with supervision most of the time. But I have been out here a lot more the past day or two. Woohoo! Yes, my playground, my long-lost piece of doggie Heaven, has been given back to me! Well, for a little while, anyway.

There is still some mud down in the right back corner, and I am going to try my best to stay away from it, so I will not get muddy and stink. Well, Mama said I stunk that one time anyways. The baths are not my favorite, but I would do almost anything to waller in that mud. I mean, play in my playground. I better play in it as much as I can today because I heard my daddy telling my mama there was another Tropical Storm coming. If that happens, my playground will be a big wet mess again! This is typical of Florida, so I have heard. We had so much debris in our yard from hurricane Ian and let's not forget all the flooding. So much that it was too dangerous for me to go out much. Mama and Daddy said we really can't complain, though, because other people got it much worse. Poor humans, I feel sorry for them and their pets. I hope this hurricane season hurries up and gets over with. I don't like all of this destruction to peoples' homes and lives. I'm going to make the best of my playground today and appreciate it because, like I have found out. Things and, most importantly, people and pets can be taken away from you in a blink of an eye. I hope everyone and their pets stay safe. I'm just going to stand here and take it all in for a minute if you don't mind, Mama, okay? I love you, Playground.

Smelling Like A Dog

So, I am so confused right now. Either my mama is losing it, or I am starting to question who and what I am right now. My mama just came up to me and hugged me, and she SNIFFED ME! When I came back inside from being out in my playground, she said, "Yona!" Yona, that's me, Yona. "You're a little damp." Then she said, "I am not going to have you smelling like a dog now." WHAT DOES THAT EVEN MEAN!?!? Does she not know I'm a DOGGIE? I have to think about this one long and hard. I mean, what am I supposed to smell like? Seriously, I don't think I am old enough to have to worry about things like this. My job is to play and make my family happy. But NO! I have to worry about how I am supposed to smell! Can someone tell me what a doggie is supposed to smell like? Since we are talking about smells. What is a human supposed to smell like? Because I have sniffed a lot of humans, and they do not all smell the same. Some smell good, and some smell, well, not so good. But then again, my opinion may be different than yours. I like certain smells that only doggies would like.

That perfume smell makes me sneeze, and my nose runs. Then there is that bathroom smell. You all know what smell I'm talking about. I don't like any smell that is associated with certain parts of a person's anatomy. Yuk.

But anyways, I have never once thought about saying to my mama, ew, you smell like a human. Go take a shower. I mean, how rude is that? But anyways, I guess I smell okay 'cause Mama didn't say I needed a bath. So that's a good sign. Right? But, if this is what I'm having to worry about now, how will it be when I am a year old? I need a nap after all this stressful thinking. Thanks a lot, Mama. We are in the middle of a storm, and all she can think about is what I smell like. I just don't get it. Smelling like a dog! why I never heard of such a thing!

Can You Say Boring Day!?!

The rain comes, and the rain goes. Then the rain comes, and then the rain goes. This is the most boringest day ever! Mama is working, and Daddy had his eyes worked on yesterday, so no one is moving around much. The workers can't come to fix the house because of all the rain. So I don't have anyone to watch me outside. My littles are home safe with their mommy, my youngest big sister Kara. My oldest big sister Kari is home sick, and I have no one to play with. I don't like the rain when it messes up my playground and keeps me from having fun. My Playground is muddy again, but it could have been a lot worse, I guess. At least I don't have a lake from this storm like I did with hurricane Ian. Hopefully, it will dry up soon. In the meantime, I'm just going to lie up here and try to take a nap. I hope to dream about my birthday party I'm going to have on the 19th of this month.

My BIG DAY is finally here, well, almost. Eight more days! Can you believe it? I hope to have lots of friends and family over. It might even be a surprise party! I'll just act really surprised when they all show up. I have been waiting for this day my whole entire life! It's going to be the best day ever! I will be a big dog then. I can't wait. But until then, I'm just going to lay right here and try to sleep this very boring day away. I saw my daddy sleeping earlier. He must be very bored too. I bet Mama would take a nap if she could too. Hopefully, tomorrow will be a better day. Sweet dreams to me, hopefully.

Enjoy today!
We can miss a lot of life
while waiting for tomorrow

Keyva, How I've Missed You So!

Keyva, I've missed you so much! Where have you been? You have been gone a long, long time. Come here and give me a big kiss! I'm glad you came over. I have grown a lot, haven't I? I am almost as tall as you are. Do you want to go play with me? We can play tug-of-war. Mama and Daddy don't like that game much because I kinda bite them sometimes by accident. Why are you looking at me like that? I said by accident. It only hurts for a minute, and I hardly ever break the skin. Well, not on Mama anyways. So, is tug-of-war a "NO," then?

Are you staying the night? Mama's letting me get on Kayle's bed now. Kayla's too, now that she has her room free of anything I might put in my mouth and swallow. But only if I am clean, though. I can't get on their beds if I am all muddy. Not even a little bit muddy even. It would be so much fun if you stayed over and we had a slumber party. You, me, Kayle, Kayla, Mama, and Daddy. We could play all kinds of games. But not board games, though, because I will run off with the little pieces and try to swallow them. Then you have to trade me a treat to get them back. Wait, on second thought, a board game might be kinda fun after all. But I know my mama would say "no," because it would be just too dangerous for me. Because I have a hard time with the word no.

But we could have ice cream. I have my very own doggie ice cream, and it is so good. I will give you a lick if you want. But just one cause you would have your own. So what do you say, Keyva? Do you want to have a slumber party?

You Scared Me!

Mama, you really shouldn't sneak up on me like that when I'm trying to counter-surf. I mean, wait patiently for food. You could make me have an accident in the house, and you know I don't do that anymore. But if I get scared bad enough, you just never know! What do you mean, "What are you doing in the Kitchen?" Would you believe me if I said I smelled your fabulous cooking and I was going to sit here patiently waiting until you gave me some of it? Emphasis on fabulous cooking.

I don't get it. How did you sneak up on me anyway? No one has ever been able to do that. I must have been pretty occupied trying to get, I mean, patiently waiting for your fabulous food to get done. See, there's that word again, fabulous. I have been anticipating every bite and how good it is going to be. I was picturing you handing me a bite each time you took a bite. Doesn't that sound like a very important bonding moment, Mama? What do you mean you're not buying any of this? I wasn't trying to sell it. I was trying to convince you I wasn't trying to counter-surf for food.

Anyways, you put up all the towels, dishcloths, and paper towels and pushed all the small appliances as far back as they would go. There is obviously nothing up there I can reach. So why would I want to go up there now anyways? So about the food that's cooking, what do you say, you feel like bonding?

My Uncle Rocky

That's my Uncle Rocky right there. My Uncle Rocky Is my Mama's baby brother. He came over to help us work in the yard because it is still a mess with all the rain and mud everywhere. My Uncle Rocky is funny. He laughs and talks a lot.

Uncle Rocky used to have really long hair, longer than my mama's, but he cut it all off. Now he has hair on his face, just like me. My mama said, "It's called a beard." He is all dirty because he has been working really, really hard trying to clean up around here. "Hey, Uncle Rocky, are you getting hot out there? Do you want to get into this cement pond and cool off? Not me, though. I don't like that cement pond! But you can if you want to."

Mama talks about how she used to play like he was her little baby, and she would rock him and feed him and play with him all the time. They are seven years apart. My Uncle Rocky's baby bed butted up to my Mama's bed when they were little, and he had a big snoopy dog that he used to climb up on and slide down it and land in my mama's bed. Mama talks about how much she loves all her brothers, and that she wouldn't trade them for anything in the world.

Mama watched Uncle Rocky a lot while they were growing up. She said she played "Mama and Baby" with him a lot, too, whatever that means. I guess, kinda like she does with me if I had to guess.

"Well, uncle Rocky let me know if you need anything, and I'll pass it on to my mama, okay?"

He has a kitty cat, but no one will let me play with it. I don't know why? I like cats. Although I have never really played with a cat before. I hear they can get real upset if you bother them.

"Hey, Uncle Rocky, try not to get too hot and sweaty and dirty out there, or Mama won't let you in the house." Or, maybe that's just me she does that way. "Well, anyways, I'll be here if you need me, okay? Oh, and if you need to dry your feet off after. I'll hold your socks for you but don't tell Mama and Daddy, okay?"

Mama, What's Wrong?

Me, my Mama and my Daddy was having a lazy afternoon. Mama was in her spot, Daddy in his spot, and of course, there was me laying in my spot minding my own business, like I ALWAYS do! When suddenly the TV turned off. I looked up at the TV and thought to myself, "How strange is this?" Then I saw my Mama leaning over onto the pillow she keeps on the couch, and HER EYES WERE CLOSED! I looked over at my Daddy, and his eyes were closed too. But to be fair, his eyes are closed A LOT! So I immediately sprung into action and ran over to my mama and propped up on her footstool, and started nudging her foot. Hey, Mama, what's wrong? Wake up? Are you all right? Do I need to call 9-1-1? But thinking to myself, I don't really know how. And if I did get an operator. What would I say? I could bark until they came to our rescue. Oh boy! I said to myself, "Yona." That's me, Yona. "Yona, just remain calm."

Then all of the sudden, Mama opened her eyes and sat up straight in her seat. That was a close call, Mama. Are you okay now? She seemed fine, so I went and laid back down. Then. She did it again! I immediately sprang back into action and jumped up on the couch, and started licking her face. She opened her eyes really fast and sat straight up again, and turned the TV back on.

Now she is shaking HER head, and looking at me really funny. I can't figure out why she keeps yawning. Why are you looking at me like that? Ummm, well, okay, and you're welcome, by the way, for me saving your life!

I think I need some doggie ice cream for that. The good kind, please. My job here is never done. Keeping an eye on Mama and Daddy and making sure they stay safe has become a full-time job. What about that ice cream now?

What's In Your Hand?

Mama, Daddy, hurry, someone's at the door. The chime is going off, and you know I'm always the first one to the door. Hurry and come open it so I can see who it is. Oh, it's Uncle Billy and Aunt Erin! I'm so happy to see you. It's been a long, long time!

Aunt Erin is like Tammy, very nice and sweet, and she pets me a lot. My uncle Billy is funny; he smiles a lot and loves to fish, but he didn't fish today. He came to see Mama and Daddy and, of course, me.

Hey Uncle Billy, whatcha got there in your hand? It looks really, really good, and it smells really, really good too. But as you know, I'm a doggie and have a very good sense of smell. I can also hear really, really good. I can see good too. I guess there is really not anything I can't do well. Me being a doggie and all. Except maybe open the doors. Well, not yet that is. But anyways, back to what you have in your hand. Are you going to finish eating that? I don't believe you are aware of the rules we have around here, so I will explain them to you. We use the command "patience," which means for me to sit and wait patiently, which I am doing right now, as you can clearly see. So, at this point, you are supposed to reward me with what's left in your hand. Only if it's not bad for me, of course.

By the looks of it, it's not. I am not upset with you or anything like that because I know you didn't really understand the rules. But now that they have been explained to you, your next step would be to give me the little bit you have left over, and I will have been rewarded for being a good girl. There you go! Thank you so much, Uncle Billy. You catch on fast.

Aunt Erin, you give the best belly rubs. I have enjoyed your visit so much. I hope you two come back soon. Unless, hey Mama, can they spend the night?

Do You Hear That, Mama?

Whoa! Hey Mama, do you hear that? Something is going on around here. I hear a lot of noise up there in the ceiling. It's so loud I bet even Daddy can hear it! I think I should go and investigate. But then again, didn't Miss Kathy tell you if you are looking for a guard dog, a Siberian Husky was not the one! So, on second thought. Maybe you and Daddy should go investigate, and I will follow close behind you, only because I'm nosey like that. I am very good at making you aware if someone is around, though. I could probably hold off a stranger by licking them continuously until you and Daddy took care of the situation. But you do know; I'm a lover, not a fighter. I haven't met one person I haven't liked yet. As a matter of fact, I haven't met any animals I haven't liked either. Not yet, anyway. I'm just that kind of doggie. I like all things.

Well, I don't like eggs or bread, though. But other than that, I think I like everything else. Well, except maybe the cement pond. I don't like the water. Speaking of water. I don't like baths either, and let's not forget about hurricanes; I really don't like them neither. But I will play in the rain and mud puddles, so go figure. But I like every other single thing.

Well, not counting the harness and leash., they are not my favorite. Neither is that new doggie food you bought me, but we'll talk about that later.

So, where were we anyway? Oh, the noise! Yes, are we going to go investigate that noise or what? We can make a game plan in case anything goes south. For those of you who don't know, that means in case anything happens to go wrong. Daddy, you go first, then Mama and I will be last, in case I need to turn around and run! I will need you all out of my way. I mean, so I can be your backup if you need me. Okay, I'm ready. Daddy lead the way! Look out, noise. Here we come.

FYI. It was just the men working on the outside of the house upstairs.

My Vanessa

This is Vanessa, she helped my Mama and me with our first book signing, and now she's helping my mama and me with a really big project. But she doesn't just help us. She helps everybody. Even people she doesn't know. My mama said Vanessa is a pure soul and has a heart of gold. My mama also said Vanessa was her daughter from another mother. That is way over my head y'all.

But anyways, my mama said she met Vanessa at a school function when she was just a little girl, and she said she fell in love with that little girl and claimed her as her own. Even though Vanessa has a wonderful mother. Mama still claims her as one of hers. Mama said Vanessa was my oldest big sister Kari's best friend. When Vanessa wasn't at our house, Kari was over at hers. Vanessa stayed here a lot. She is part of our family. My mama said Vanessa is a very special person. One that you would be proud to call a friend. In fact, my Mama said Vanessa went from being this little girl she loved so dearly to being one of her dearest friends. Vanessa dedicates her time to helping so many people all the time, and she loves doing it. She said that's just how I am; I love helping people. That my friends is not taught, it's built inside you way down deep. It's a calling not everyone has.

Anyways, today is a very important day because my mama and I have been asked to go talk to the kids at an elementary school, and Mama is going to read some of our books to them. Mama has never spoken in front of a lot of people before. So Vanessa being the person she is, is going to come help my mama. They spent hours last night putting together a presentation. Whatever that is. But anyways, wish us luck. I know I'm going to have a blast. A whole school of "Littles" that's right up my alley. Thank you, Vanessa, for helping My mama and me. I love you!

My One Year Birthday, Part One!

Happy Birthday To Me! Happy Birthday To Me! Happy birthday, dear Yona, THAT'S ME! Happy birthday To me! Guess what today is? You guessed it; IT'S MY 1ST BIRTHDAY! How did you guess? What gave it away? Just kidding! I am so excited! What a day it is going to be.

First thing this morning is my book signing, where I will get to meet all my friends and sign my books, and get petted... a lot!. Don't forget the petting part; that's important. And pictures! Lots and lots of pictures. All of my four-legged friends are having their photos taken with party hats on for me for my birthday and then! I'm so excited!

Then, it's birthday party time, and it's all for me! It's going to take me two days to complete my birthday because I know I cannot fit this big exciting day into just one day. I still have lots and lots to do. Well, my Mama and Tammy have lots and lots to do anyway, because I am the birthday girl, after all.

A lot of my family and my furry friends are going to come from all over just to see me on my very important special day.

Pictures, cake, ice cream, presents, and friends, both two-legged and four-legged will be there. Mama said no balloons, though. Well, not too many, anyway. I will have to update you all tomorrow about how good it went, and show you all the pictures. Woohoo! My big day has finally arrived. To be continued...

YONA
That's
me!

My One-Year Birthday Grand Finale

Well, my first birthday was a big success, and I am the happiest, luckiest puppy in all the whole wide world. I thought the monthly birthdays were great, and they were. But this "FIRST YEAR" birthday was the best day ever! Just look at all my friends and family!

My youngest big sister Kara made me my very own homemade birthday cake! I better be careful and not try and eat it all at once, or I might get a belly ache. But I'm going to eat as much as my Mama and Daddy will let me, that's for sure. It's MY birthday cake, after all. Woohoo! I would share, but no one seems to want any of mine. They bought their own cake made for humans. Mine is a special doggie cake. Or should I say DOG now?

A couple of my friends stopped by during my book signing, and we had our pictures taken together. They are so nice, and I love them.

I would also like to give a big shout-out to Darlene at Pet World in Auburndale, for allowing us to have our book signing in your wonderful establishment. Thank you so much!

Then we all came home after the book signing, and I took a nap while Mama and Tammy went shopping to pick up some last-minute party favors. AND THEN IT WAS PARTY TIME!!! Pizza, cake, ice cream, and PRESENTS, PRESENTS, PRESENTS.

Thank you to everyone who wished me happy birthday, sent pictures, and came to my party! I have had the best year and am so thankful you have allowed us to come into your homes each morning and share all of our adventures with you. I hope you have enjoyed it as much as we have. It's been a wonderful ten months, and I am thankful to you all.

This may be the last entry of my last book, but I hope I always stay in your hearts. As I know, you all will forever stay in mine. Stay safe, love life, and live it to the fullest. I know I am. Love you, my friends.

Goodbye! Your friend Yona! 🐾

Yona's Birthday Scrapbook

LITA

TOBY

Bridget

BRADY

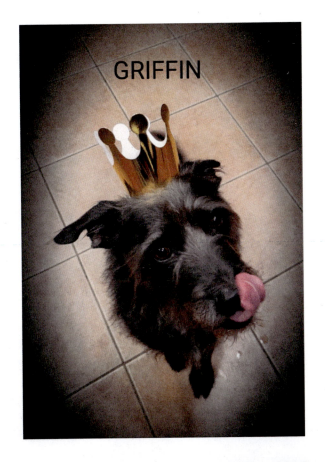

GRIFFIN

HELP!

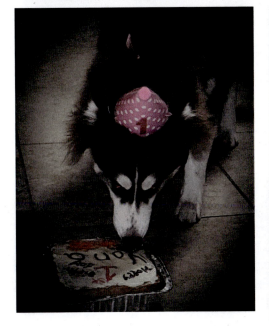

A Giant Thank You

I am now one whole year old. I have learned a lot from my short time on this earth. I have learned to "sit," "come," and "patience." I've learned how to go outside to take care of my business. I have learned how to wear my harness without chewing on it. I don't jump up as much as I did unless I am really excited. I learned dogs do not belong on kitchen counters. Hey, don't judge me; I am a dog after all! A real, whole, year-old dog! At least, that's what I'm calling myself now. How exciting is that!

Some may say I'm still just a pup. But I am claiming "dog status," woohoo! Am I perfect? Absolutely not, but I have never had an accident in the house since I learned how to go outside. But most importantly, I have learned human-to-pet interaction. I have learned how to treat people kindly, and how I should be treated. I have learned the importance of family and friendship.

All the friends I have met on this journey are my greatest achievement, and I love you all. I have felt happiness, confusion, pain, and sadness, and how to deal with each phase of them. I have feelings just like you, and I do my best to comfort and help those in need just like you would. I know the importance of family and what it means to be a part of one.

I have learned it takes hard work and dedication to keep a family or any relationship together and from both sides. You get out of it what you put in it. Get what you give, in other words.

I would also like to thank Jennifer Parker for editing portions of this book and Jordan Parker for creating book video trailers.

My books are not perfect! They are a homemade version of my life with my new family. We did not have rehearsals. We just came as we were with messy hair and play clothes, and yes, sometimes the house was not perfect. It was not staged, just like my life is not staged. This was real-life, raw footage of a puppy in her new home. There's no actors in this book. Just a loving family and their dog, me, Yona! I hope you enjoyed it as much as I enjoyed participating in it for you. Me and my Littles, of course. I am so happy you let me share my home and my family with you. I did hear through the grapevine that there may be a yearly addition, so stay tuned. Again, Love you all!

Your faithful friend,
    Yona 🐾

About Karen

(Yona's Mommy)

Karen Olive is a wife, mother, and grandmother to three grandchildren, Matthew, Kayle, and Kayla. She is a full-time nurse. Out of a difficult season of grief, she started posting on Facebook the pictures and adventures of Yona her puppy, a Siberian Husky.

From these posts, people started following Yona's adventures and sharing them with their friends. Never thinking about writing a book, her friends encouraged her to think about it. Well, the rest is history.

Please follow Yona, Mommy and Daddy, and the "Littles," on Facebook:
https://www.facebook.com/YonaSiberianHusky
Please share this book with your friends, and anyone you know who is a dog lover, and needs to smile (Hello, that is everyone!), we thank you for your love and support!

What People are Saying:

Yona...a great read!
This is a wonderful story about a Siberian Husky. It is about her adventures growing up...lessons she learned and lessons she taught her mommy and daddy!
It is funny and a great read...you will enjoy her adventures!
Mary Dunson

Such a fun beautiful book!
This is such a cute book. Full of fun adventures of Yona a beautiful Siberian husky! The stories are perfect for anyone, I can't wait to read some of the stories to my grandchildren.
Brandon Bagwell

A Truly Delightful Book!
For those who need uplifted, I feel this book will be especially welcomed, bringing comfort and joy. Whether as a treat for yourself, or gift for a loved one, once captivated by Yona, books two and three will surely be eagerly awaited! Karen Turner Olive's beautiful writing style is a sheer pleasure to read. Join in the fun, as the gorgeous Yona warmly invites you into her wonderful world!
Laura Maxwell, author and radio show host. (Scotland).

Heartfelt Adventures
The Adventures of Yona is such a heartfelt book that makes you see life through the eyes of a puppy! Young Yona summing up life in her forever home from day one to now... When you are having a bad day or just want an

extra smile this book will bring daily joy to life! My 9-year-old granddaughter is enjoying the book as well.
Serena Lear

Is a wonderful read. Can't wait for more.
Karen does an amazing job at capturing the views of Yona. I have really enjoyed reading the book. I can't wait to see more. I've never met Yona But by Karen's description I sure feel like I know her. Yona is so beautiful And I know she has a beautiful soul. Can't wait for the other books
Ann Russell

Makes me smile
Yona makes me smile! I love reading her daily puppy adventures. Having been through puppyhood with my own dogs, Yona's antics bring back fond memories and lots of laughs! Dogs can really heal your heart when you are hurting and so can reading their stories! Thanks Yona, for helping me through some of my own stressful days!
J. Nixon

Great book that the whole family can enjoy!
This book brings you inside the life of a Siberian Husky named Yona! The moment you start reading, I assure you, you will fall in love with her! She's learning what it's like to be a puppy in Florida with a wonderful forever family! It's heartwarming, quirky, adventurous, and fun! Great read for adults and children!
Kimberly Roy

I absolutely love this book!
Karen did a great job. You will be carried away with Yona's stories and look forward to each new day.
Lori Cook

A Good morning read
I look forward to hearing from Yona each day about her daily adventures. I highly recommend this book to anyone that is a pet lover.
Tammy Olive

Yona's fun, adventurous, and loved
I love reading Yona's adventures because her days are interesting and there is so much humor in everything she does.
This book is excellent for everyone to enjoy and you can read it to your children.
Yona is a beautiful and intelligent puppy who is loved and cared for.
Robyn Rasmussen

The Adventures of Yona is such an uplifting book!
Seeing the world through the eyes of a Siberian Husky is very interesting and entertaining! You won't regret reading this gem!
Selma Gandy

Must read!
Great book for the whole family! Never a dull moment with sweet yona.
Kara

Yona's daily adventures make me laugh.
Keep in up Yona!
Leo Raymond

A Little Break From the Mundane
A sweet book of adventure and shenanigans! Yona is a pup full of life and curiosity.
This story is a great and wonderful break from the real world that is currently at odds.

It was like taking little mini vacations reading this gem of a story!
I highly recommend.
Sandie

Yona's Adventures

Yona's adventures make me smile. It's like my coffee in the morning it starts my day off right.
Yona stories have helped heal my broken heart. July 4th will be 1 year without my sweet Sadie girl. She lived 9 and half years. She was my friend and companion. She' truly missed . Yona fills a void in my ❤️
Jessie Melton

So much fun with sweet Yona

Yonas stories are so much fun. She brings a smile to my face with each new adventure. You won't be disappointed.
Janet O.

Yona's Adventures are the Best ❗💯❤️😃

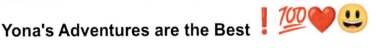

The Best book ❗ ❗ 💗💯 So sweet, entertaining, and encouraging, and puts a Very Bright Spot in my day every day. I look forward to reading it every day, and it brings me Joy. I highly recommend this book to everyone ❗ ❗
💕 You will be so glad you read it, just like me. 😍 It will make your day ❗ ❗ 😊
Lisa Flora

Great Book

Yona is just too cute.
GatorTech of Winter Haven

Great book! Uplifting.
You must read about Yona, she is the smartest Siberian Husky and so beautiful! You will enjoy reading this book!!
Tammy Roberts

Yona the Siberian Husky
A great read following Yona the Siberian Husky each day. Karen Turner Olive has such an engaging style of writing that makes for a feel-good experience. Love this.
Redd

Great family book
The adventures of Yona is a great read for adults and children. It is written so well and is definitely one of a kind. Highly recommend!!!!
Dena

I love following Yona's adventures and Karen
Loved these daily experiences with Yona.
Jane Sherepita

Love reading about Yona
Love reading about Yona, and her weekly adventures. She is very beautiful. She's so exciting to watch. I know that She holds a very special place in the lives of her family members. I'm in anticipation to experience more of her life.
Adrena Hamilton

Great daily read. Makes you laugh and smile. Never a dull moment!
Bonnie McCain

I can't help but smile when I'm scrolling through my page and see Yona's silly face. You have to stop and see

what Shenanigans she is up to now. Her stories are always a refreshing part of my day, love me some Yona!
Kari Fyock

I read Yona's posts first thing in the morning before getting ready for work. Her shenanigans make me smile and start my day off feeling optimistic. My boys love hearing her daily stories as well.
Chandler Fox

Get yours

FREE GIFT

With book purchase

**Autographed
Photo
of Yona**

Write to KarenROlive@aol.com

YONA MECH

MORE COMING SOON

JOIN FACEBOOK
FIND OUT FIRST

https://www.facebook.com/YonaSiberianHusky

Made in the USA
Columbia, SC
06 December 2022

72821374R00095